IMAGES
of America

CLEVELAND
1930–2000

(*cover*) CLEVELAND: AN ALL-AMERICAN CITY. This was downtown Cleveland in 1949, the year it was named an All-American City. Streetcars and trackless trolleys crisscrossed Ontario and Superior Avenues as pedestrians filled Public Square, the heart of the city. In the center is the Soldiers and Sailors Monument behind which stand the Williamson Building, the tallest building, and to the left is the Cuyahoga Building. In 1982, these buildings were imploded (see images on page 121) to make way for the BP (British Petroleum) Building skyscraper. (Photograph by Carl McDow.)

IMAGES
of America

CLEVELAND
1930–2000

Thea Gallo Becker

ARCADIA
PUBLISHING

Published by Arcadia Publishing
Charleston, South Carolina

Library of Congress Catalog Card Number: 2004115894

For all general information contact Arcadia Publishing at:
Telephone 843-853-2070
Fax 843-853-0044
E-mail sales@arcadiapublishing.com
For customer service and orders:
Toll-Free 1-888-313-2665

Visit us on the Internet at www.arcadiapublishing.com

For my beautiful daughter, Thealexa.

CONTENTS

ACKNOWLEDGMENTS

The photographs used in this book were obtained primarily from Cleveland State University Library Special Collections, William C. Barrow, Special Collections librarian. My sincere thanks and appreciation goes to the staff for allowing me to browse through the images and select only the best for this publication. CSU's Special Collections area is an outstanding repository of photographs and clippings from *The Cleveland Press*, once this city's finest newspaper. In order to give the credit deserved to the *Press* photographers for the outstanding images that fill the pages of this book, the name of the individual photographer will appear after the image where possible. Every attempt was made to properly credit each photograph. In the event no name could be associated with an image, no credit will appear, as the image is part of Special Collections. Some images will bear the name of photographers not affiliated with the *Press*, and they are noted. I would like to especially thank Mr. David Kachinko, whose outstanding photographs of Cleveland in the 1990s helped to complete my visual history.

Among the many books available on Cleveland history, I found the following to be most useful in compiling the text: *Cleveland: The Making of a City*, by William Ganson Rose, 1950; *The Encyclopedia of Cleveland History*, edited by David Van Tassel and John J. Grabowski, 1987; and *Cleveland TV Memories*, by Tom Feran and R.D. Heldenfels, 1999. Finally, the *Press* newspaper clippings provided abundant primary source material.

Many of the images used in the compilation of Cleveland's history may be found on the Cleveland Memory website: *http://web.ulib.csuohio.edu/speccoll/*.

INTRODUCTION

This book is the second volume in the visual history of Cleveland, taking up where the first edition ended—with the construction of Cleveland's most famous landmark, the Terminal Tower. Cleveland's history is presented in a chronological manner with several chapters devoted to areas of special interest like sports or the arts. Compiling the photographs to be used for post-1930 Cleveland was especially challenging since any one topic, post-World War II recovery for example, generated enough images to fill a single volume. In selecting my images, I strove to tell a story, and at the same time, to be entertaining. Some of the images selected were not my first choice, but the story behind them was too important to omit.

As Cleveland was one of the major cities in North America, everybody who was anybody passed through, many leaving an indelible imprint. Those of the Baby Boom generation still remember when The Beatles played in Cleveland, with ticket prices as little as $5. And who could forget the debut of Elvis Presley at Brooklyn High School before Elvis, "The King," was born. There was a time when Cleveland topped the list not only of entertainers, but also politicians, social activists, writers, investors, and others who wanted a major venue to launch their particular vision.

In 1936, Cleveland was chosen to host the Great Lakes Exposition, which attracted thousands of visitors. At the time, Cleveland's population topped 900,000, making it the fifth largest city in America. Cleveland had celebrated the opening of the Terminal Tower and Union Terminal; dedicated a new concert hall, Severance Hall, for its orchestra; and welcomed its new municipal lakefront stadium. Clevelanders watched with pride as one of their own, Jesse Owens, won four gold medals at the 1936 Olympics in Berlin. The Cleveland Barons and the Cleveland Rams entertained sports fans, and the National Air Races thrilled everyone. The 1930s presented a darker side as well, with the Great Depression forcing one-third of Clevelanders to lose their jobs and homes. The first public housing projects were constructed, as were two new high-level bridges.

World War II brought many changes to Cleveland as civic leaders and industries teamed together to make Cleveland's wartime accomplishments unsurpassed. Many citizens answered the call to fight, leaving their families behind, and many women entered the work force for the first time, ably filling positions usually reserved for their male counterparts. Many will remember how the war was interrupted by a disaster closer to home, the East Ohio Gas Explosion, which claimed lives and leveled homes and businesses. Post-war recovery brought Cleveland a few new titles. In 1948, the Cleveland Indians won the World Series, and in 1949, Cleveland was named an All-American City. During the 1950s, Cleveland weathered two paralyzing storms, modernized highways and transportation, and began to think seriously about urban renewal.

The 1960s brought many changes to Cleveland, like the construction of Erieview to stem the spread of urban blight. Two new urban universities were opened, Cleveland State University and Cuyahoga Community College, making higher learning accessible and affordable for everyone. And history was made when Carl B. Stokes was elected the first African-American mayor of a major American city. Cleveland had survived riots and shoot-outs, and when the decade closed, a new course was set for the city.

Cleveland made political history yet again by electing Dennis Kucinich mayor, the youngest ever of a major American city. He beat a recall election, and default kept him from winning a second term. RTA was established, the Cleveland Ballet gave its first performance, and public schools were ordered desegregated. While it was no longer a top-ten city, President Jimmy Carter and Republican challenger Ronald Reagan found Cleveland the ideal location for their national debate.

Through the years, Cleveland has seen it all and provided enough challenges to be met for many years to come. Cleveland still remains a wonderful location to live and to work, a fun place to relax and to be entertained—and is a city with great potential for the future.

–Thea Gallo Becker

LAKE ERIE SUNSET. This hauntingly serene image of fishermen at East 72nd Street and Lakeshore Boulevard was taken in 1956, a time in Cleveland that mirrored the calm reflected in this scene. (Photograph by Bernie Noble.)

One

THRIVING IN
THE THIRTIES

WELCOME TO CLEVELAND! A lighthouse is poised at the mouth of the Cuyahoga River with the Cleveland skyline in the distance. Standing above everything else is Cleveland's newest landmark, the historic Terminal Tower, at the time the tallest building between New York City and Chicago. Cleveland's skyline would change dramatically over the years, leaving the Terminal Tower the giant no more.

THE TERMINAL TOWER, CLEVELAND'S NEWEST LANDMARK. On June 28, 1930, the new Union Terminal was dedicated. It was built at a cost of $150 million and employed over 500 office workers. The transportation terminal was situated below the tower itself, which had been completed by 1928. Terminal Tower stood over 700 feet above the station concourse and had 52 floors, including an observation deck. (Photograph by Frank Reed.)

INSIDE THE TERMINAL TOWER. As soon as visitors passed through the brass-plated glass doors to enter the Terminal Tower, they were surrounded by ornate, high-arched ceilings and marble floors. The lobby remains much the same as it looked in this 1939 photograph, when a trip to Public Square in downtown Cleveland was a treat. Graham Anderson, Probst & White, a Chicago architectural firm, designed the Terminal Tower.

DEDICATION OF THE TERMINAL TOWER. Dedication ceremonies to mark the official opening of the new transportation terminal were held in the station concourse and were attended by hundreds of local and national dignitaries. Two people who were most conspicuously absent from the occasion were brothers Mantis James and Oris Paxton Van Sweringen, the visionary businessmen who were responsible for the building of the landmark Cleveland Union Terminal Complex.

RETAILERS WELCOME THE TERMINAL TOWER. The opening of the new Cleveland Union Terminal Complex, arguably the finest of any American city at the time, was cause for a citywide celebration. Here, the May Company department store was decorated with banners. This busy retail strip included the F.W. Woolworth Company, Bailey's Department Store, and Richman's, all of which have since closed. Cleveland, once a retailer's mecca, has no major department stores downtown today.

11

CLEVELAND CELEBRATES ITS 134TH ANNIVERSARY! In July of 1930, members of Cleveland's City Club, (left to right) Warren M. Briggs, Bernard S. Brady, and R.G. Beattie, prepared to lay a wreath at the foot of the statue of General Moses Cleaveland, the city's namesake and founder, who arrived in 1796 as part of a surveying party. The monument to Moses Cleaveland still remains on the southwest quadrant of Public Square.

(below) **THE HIGBEE COMPANY.** Anchoring the Terminal Tower complex on Ontario Avenue and Public Square was the Higbee Company department store, photographed here in 1934. The Higbee Company would remain one of Cleveland's and Northeast Ohio's major retailers for several decades. Higbee's was sold in 1987 to Dillard Department Stores, and in 1992, it was renamed "Dillard's."

TAYLOR'S DEPARTMENT STORE. Another major Cleveland department store was Taylor's. When it first opened in the late 19th century, it was known as William Taylor Son and Company. The store was located at 630 Euclid Avenue and stood nine stories tall. When this photograph was taken in 1934, the store had completed renovations totaling half a million dollars and had shortened its name to Taylor's Department Store. In 1961, Taylor's closed its doors.

THE HALLE BROTHERS COMPANY. In its heyday, Cleveland was home to many of the largest, most lucrative retailers in the business. The Halle Brothers Company, seen here on Euclid Avenue, together with the May Company and the Higbee Company, completed the trio of popular shopping destinations for downtown visitors. When this photograph was taken in 1936, Halle's had already opened several branch stores in neighboring suburbs, a move soon followed by its competitors.

13

REVIVING THE OFFICE OF MAYOR. The bronze statue of Tom L. Johnson, who was long considered by many to be Cleveland's finest mayor, was given a thorough scrubbing by Charles Hagedorn and Frank Straka. Located in the northwest quadrant of Public Square, the statue's revival in the 1930s coincided with the return of the mayoral form of government and the abandonment of the city manager form of government.

THE CITY MANAGER AND THE MAYOR. Daniel E. Morgan (1877–1949), on the left, became the last city manager of Cleveland when in 1932 Raymond T. Miller (1893–1966), on the right, was elected mayor of the city. Here, Morgan is congratulating Miller as he prepares to leave the office of city manager, which he had held since 1930. Miller served as mayor for a single two-year term and lost a re-election bid to Harry Davis, who assumed the office of mayor in 1934.

PRESIDENT HOOVER VISITS CLEVELAND. In October of 1930, President Herbert Hoover (center) appeared on Public Square flanked by his wife and John D. Marshall, who served at the time as mayor of Cleveland under the city manager plan of government, which empowered the manager to oversee the day-to-day operations of the city and left the mayor to assume lesser ministerial duties.

FDR's PRESIDENTIAL VISIT TO CLEVELAND. As a major American city, Cleveland always topped the list of cities to visit for every president and for all presidential candidates. In 1936, during the Great Lakes Exposition, downtown Public Square was crowded with onlookers hoping to get a glimpse of President Franklin D. Roosevelt as his motorcade rounded the Soldiers and Sailors Monument, as seen in the upper right corner.

THE LORAIN-CARNEGIE BRIDGE. One of the most impressive civic building projects in Cleveland was the construction of the Lorain-Carnegie Bridge. Completed in 1932, this new high-level bridge followed the construction of the Detroit-Superior high-level bridge, which was the first built across the Cuyahoga River more than a decade earlier. The Lorain-Carnegie Bridge was designed to link Lorain Avenue and Central Avenue for easier travel. Looking north along the Cuyahoga River, this view shows the Lorain-Carnegie Bridge under construction. It was made exclusively of steel and concrete and spanned a mile in length. Engineers Wilbur J. Watson & Associates designed the bridge with assistance from architect Frank Walker. The finishing touch on the bridge was the completion of four huge stone figures holding various examples of transportation. From 1980 to 1983, the Lorain-Carnegie Bridge was closed for extensive renovation. When it reopened, it had been renamed the Hope Memorial Bridge in honor of the father of entertainer and Clevelander Bob Hope. His father was a stonemason who worked on the bridge.

CLEVELAND MUNICIPAL STADIUM. In July of 1931, Cleveland unveiled its new sports and entertainment stadium on the lakefront. Cleveland Municipal Stadium, when completed, would accommodate a crowd of nearly 78,200, making it the largest outdoor stadium at the time. The first event staged there was a boxing match on July 3rd between Max Schmeling and Young Stribling. In this photograph, preparations are being made for the Summer Opera Festival to be held at the end of the month.

THE INAUGURAL SUMMER OPERA FESTIVAL. During the week of July 28th to August 2nd of 1931, Cleveland Municipal Stadium was the site of an outdoor opera festival sponsored by *The Cleveland Press*, Cleveland's leading newspaper. The event filled the stadium to capacity and drew many who normally frequented Severance Hall for an evening concert. Wearing his trademark round specs is Newton D. Baker, former Cleveland mayor and secretary of war under President Wilson. The program featured *Aida* with tickets selling for $1 and $2 apiece.

THE GREAT LAKES EXPOSITION. From June 27 to October 4, 1936, Cleveland hosted the first season of the international Great Lakes Exposition, which was held on the lakefront in front of the Cleveland Municipal Stadium. Seen here (left to right) is Mayor Harold H. Burton; Winette Kronz; the legendary Eddie Cantor, receiving the key to the exposition; and Lincoln Dickey. At the time this photograph was taken, Mayor Burton was serving the first of three consecutive terms.

AERIAL VIEW OF THE GREAT LAKES EXPOSITION. The compactness of the Great Lakes Exposition and its central location in Cleveland, fronting Lake Erie, is seen here. Downtown Cleveland and its newest landmark, the Terminal Tower, can be seen in the background. In the foreground, the entrance to the exposition and the central buildings on the grounds can be seen. The second season of the Great Lakes Exposition would begin May 29, 1937.

SEASON ONE OF THE GREAT LAKES EXPOSITION. Visitors are leaving the Florida exhibit and the Firestone Fountain as crowds move under the East 9th Street underpass to the amusement zone and the Midway. While the blimps glided by overhead like giant silver cigars, the voice of the announcer could be heard by all.

ADMIRAL BYRD'S SHIP VISITS DURING SEASON TWO. The Great Lakes Exposition was visited during its second season in 1937 by Admiral Byrd's ship. The Goodyear Blimp can be seen hovering above, while the Terminal Tower appears to rise out of the Midway.

THE MAIN STREET BRIDGE. The northern-most motor vehicle and pedestrian bridge built across the Cuyahoga River was the low-level Main Street Bridge. It was originally built following Cleveland's annexation of Ohio City in 1854 to help handle the increased traffic of people and goods across the Cuyahoga River Valley. By the 1930s, the increased motor traffic combined with the frequent interruptions by river traffic led to the bridge being replaced by the high-level Main Avenue Bridge.

MAIN STREET BRIDGE AND MAIN AVENUE BRIDGE. Construction of the high-level Main Avenue Bridge can be seen on the Cuyahoga River in 1939. Planning for a new high-level bridge to replace the low-level Main Street Bridge began in 1930 with financing coming primarily from the WPA. With nearly one-third of Clevelanders left jobless due to the Great Depression, the construction of a new bridge was welcomed.

MAIN AVENUE BRIDGE CONSTRUCTION. Work crews in May of 1939 prepared to place the first steel girder connecting the east and west halves of the high-level Main Avenue Bridge over the Cuyahoga River Valley. After a series of emergency repairs throughout the 1980s, the bridge was closed from 1990 to 1992 for major renovation.

MAIN AVENUE BRIDGE DECK CONSTRUCTION. West of the Main Avenue Bridge, in June of 1939, work crews were seen laying the bridge deck. The bridge, when completed, consisted of eight truss-cantilever spans of varying lengths with additional bridgework at the end joining it to the Shoreway. With a total length of 2,250 feet, the bridge, with its approaches, would be more than a mile in length.

THE GREAT DEPRESSION HITS CLEVELAND. On the cold winter afternoon of February 18, 1930, Cleveland's unemployed gathered on Public Square for free hot coffee and rolls from Mrs. Albert Schmidt (right), a famous cook who also helped prepare meals at the Geneva Peace Conference. Describing herself as a "friend of humanity," Mrs. Schmidt hoped to get all the restaurants in Cleveland to cooperate and feed the needy until they could feed themselves.

APPLES FOR THE HUNGRY. In November of 1937, as the Great Depression showed no signs of ending, a long line of people carrying straw baskets lined up at East 51st Street and Superior Avenue. They came to fill their baskets with government surplus apples. Workers prepared to distribute the surplus commodity to the needy. For some, apples were all they had to eat for the day.

NEIGHBORS PROTEST EVICTION. For many, the Great Depression resulted not only in a loss of employment, but as a consequence, a loss of homes as well. A crowd of neighbors and other supporters gather on the west side in front of the modest two-family dwelling of Joseph Sparanga to protest his eviction for failure to pay his mortgage. It was a real concern, as many who came to protest wondered if they might be next. (Photograph provided by the Everett Collection.)

LAKEVIEW TERRACE. The first public housing project authorized by the federal government was built on a 22-acre site located at West 28th Street between Lake Erie and the Main Avenue Bridge. Completed in 1937, Lakeview Terrace was one of three housing projects. The others were the Cedar-Central Apartments and Outhwaite Homes, planned and built over a four-year period at a cost of $10 million. The result provided homes for 2,000 Cleveland families.

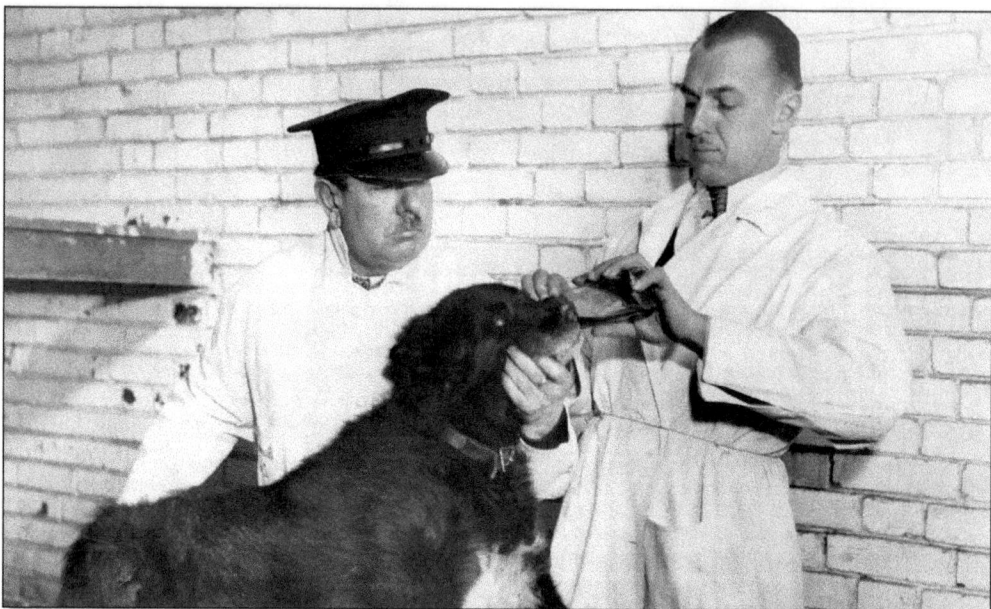

BALTO. Balto is being examined by Veterinarian W.T. Brinker and Zookeeper Curly Wilson in this photograph. The most popular animals at the Cleveland Zoo in the 1930s were Balto and six members of the sled dog team that had delivered life-saving diphtheria serum to Nome, Alaska, in 1925. They were brought to Cleveland through a public fundraising campaign, heavily underwritten by the nickels and dimes of Cleveland school children. The campaign raised over $2,300 to purchase the dogs and bring them to the Cleveland Zoo.

THE HIPPODROME THEATER. This is a 1939 view of Cleveland's popular Hippodrome Theater, located on East 7th and Euclid Avenue. The Hippodrome began as a playhouse, and later abandoned live theater and underwent extensive remodeling to feature only movies. Of all the movie theaters in Cleveland, the Hippodrome was arguably the finest and the most popular. It was also the last theater in the city to close.

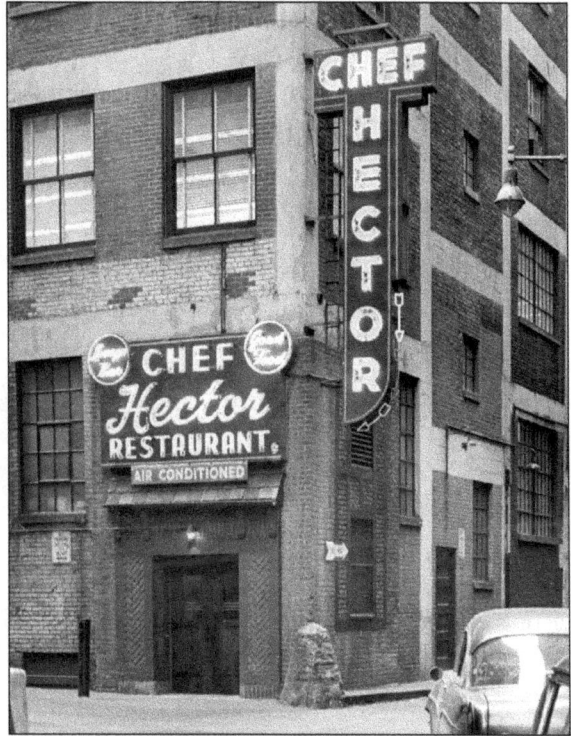

CHEF BOY-AR-DEE. Local restaurateur and chef, Hector Boiardi, opened his first restaurant in Cleveland in 1924. The reputation of his spaghetti dinners led Boiardi to start producing dinners containing dry spaghetti, a can of his secret sauce, and packet of Parmesan cheese. It was sold in grocery stores under the name of "Chef Boy-Ar-Dee." From 1931–1967, Boiardi operated Chef Boiardi's Restaurant on Prospect Avenue, which was later changed to Chef Hector's after the spaghetti business was sold. (Photograph by Bill Nehez.)

THE NEIGHBORHOOD OF LITTLE ITALY. This is a view of Mayfield Road looking east from Murray Hill Road—the heart of Little Italy. Cleveland is a city of many nationalities, and at one time, each had their own neighborhood, claiming certain portions of the city as their own. The Italians had five areas spread throughout Cleveland. Little Italy remains perhaps the most popular neighborhood, attracting many tourists to the now-historic area.

THE TORSO MURDERS. The most infamous unsolved crimes to haunt Cleveland in the late 1930s were the "Torso Murders," so-named because all that remained of the dismembered victims was the torso—their heads were removed, and if found, were not near the body. The crimes occurred in an area called Kingsbury Run near the Cuyahoga River. Here, Fire Warden Patrick Barrett, in the shack located under Superior Viaduct, examines the area for clues as Sergeant Victor Webber looks on.

SAFETY DIRECTOR ELIOT NESS. Eliot Ness (far right) came to Cleveland in 1935 to become safety director at the invitation of Senator Harold Burton (left). Ness gained fame in Chicago with his law enforcement team, "The Untouchables," because they would not succumb to the temptation of corruption. It was Burton's need to clean up the Cleveland police department that prompted the call to Ness. In the center is Edward Blythin, who succeeded Burton as mayor. (Photograph by John Nash.)

Two

WAR AND INDUSTRY

CLEVELANDERS READY FOR WAR. When the United States entered World War II in 1941, Cleveland was ready to fulfill its duty and sent anywhere from 3,000 to 5,000 men and women, by some estimates, to fill the service ranks. Here, a group of inductees with an accompanying marching band pose in front of Cleveland Municipal Stadium as they wait to board the trains that would carry them to their assigned training camps. (Photograph by Herman Seid.)

LANGSTON HUGHES. Not all voices called for war. Langston Hughes (1902–1967), on the right, appeared at a meeting of the League Against War and Fascism in Public Hall. As one of the most influential and celebrated African-American writers of the time, Hughes lent his support to those opposed to war. Hughes came to Cleveland when he was a teenager and began writing poetry, then plays and novels. He was a gifted orator who would also use his talents in the Civil Rights Movement.

FROM THE ARMORY TO EUROPE. Rows of young draftees waited in the Central Armory located at East 6th Street and Lakeside Avenue before they marched down to the Cleveland Union Terminal on Public Square to board the trains that would take them to their assignments. New recruits were usually treated to a parade as crowds gathered to cheer them on and say one last goodbye.

CALLING ALL CLEVELANDERS. Standing at the foot of a long staircase is a group of approximately 40 army reservists, many of them fathers, waiting to leave Cleveland for their new assignments. At the time, Cleveland had some 50 draft boards manned by hundreds of volunteers.

COLLEGE STUDENTS PROTEST THE WAR. Student war protestors are often associated with the Vietnam War, but here, a crowd of protestors, many of them students, assemble and march at Case Western Reserve University in University Circle. The banner reads, "The Law School Strikes Against War and Fascism." Those who refused the call to serve ended up trading a dorm room for a jail cell.

WAR BOND RALLY. Frank Lausche (second from left) served as mayor from 1941–1944. Here, he greets Mrs. Mark Clark, the featured speaker at the May Company's week-long Four Freedoms Bond Show and the wife of U.S. Army General Mark Clark. Also appearing at the May 1943 rally were Army Captain and Big Band leader Glenn Miller (left) and Army Corp Major Allen Martini, veteran of 27 bombing missions over Nazi Germany.

STAGE DOOR CANTEEN. After graduating from Shaw High School, Cleveland native Eleanor Parker joined the Pasadena (California) Playhouse and went on to become a movie star. On August 21, 1943, Miss Parker returned to Cleveland as the guest of honor at the Stage Door Canteen for American servicemen. This was Miss Parker's third appearance at the Stage Door Canteen, and she was presented with the scroll as tribute for her work on behalf of the servicemen.

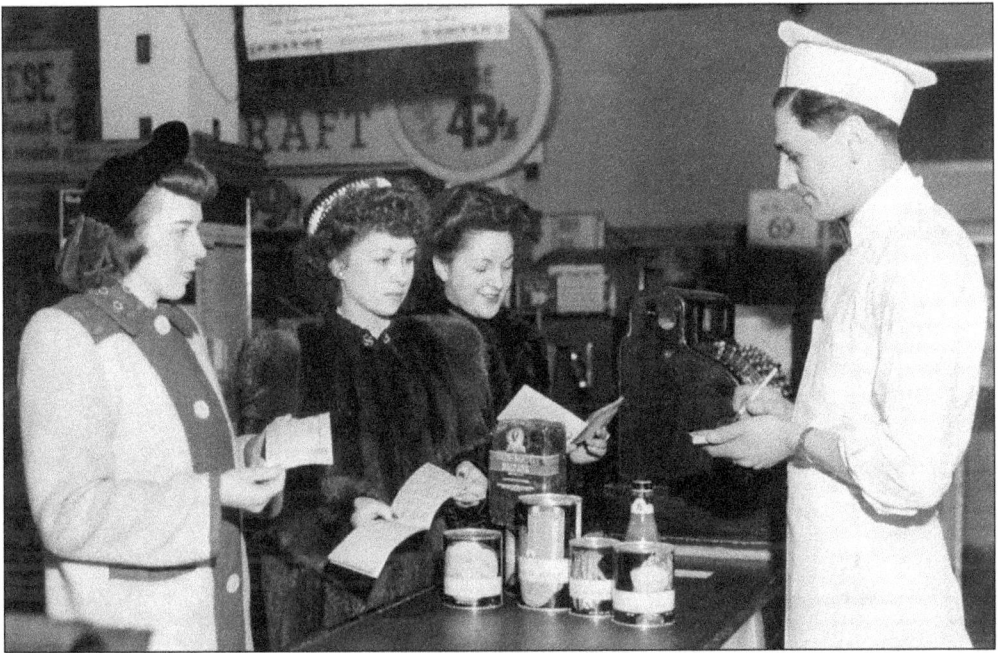

CLEVELANDERS RATIONING FOR WAR. War rationing was common during WWII, as seen in this photograph taken in 1943. Kroger grocery store clerk Russell Younglass waited on a trio of customers as they flipped through their ration books to find the required stamps needed to purchase the goods at the counter. (Photograph by James Meli.)

CHILDREN SUPPORT THE WAR EFFORT. Young students at Hodge Elementary School at East 74th Street, on the east side, stand proudly in front of a mountain of newspapers they helped to collect from neighbors and businesses in an effort to do their part in supporting the war. Paper drives were one of the most popular fundraising drives used by students, even well after the war. (Photograph by James Meli.)

SAILORS AT GM. The war effort provided a chance for Clevelanders who were hit hard by the Great Depression to work again, as area industries recalled workers, hired new ones, and trained servicemen to use their machinery. Here, on December 19, 1940, a group of sailors listen to a representative of the General Motors Corporation at the Cleveland Diesel Engine Plant on Coit Road, which produced gun and tank parts and engines.

THE WAR SENDS WOMEN OFF TO WORK. "Rosie the Riveter" may have been a promotional character, but women in Cleveland really did enter the work force, and in large numbers as the war machine gained momentum. At the General Motors Diesel Engine Plant in January of 1942, Mrs. Jeanne Hall (left) and Miss Rose Saladina (right) are among the thousands of women who joined the work force. Mrs. Hall is wearing slacks, something new in women's fashion and brought about by the rationing of nylon for stockings.

PRODUCTION OF WAR MATERIALS. In 1943, the large Cleveland Fisher Body Plant had been totally converted from peacetime production of automobiles to wartime production. Here, one section of the plant that was used in making machine parts for diesel engines is seen. The plant was also in the tooling stage for the production of aircraft parts and sub-assemblies.

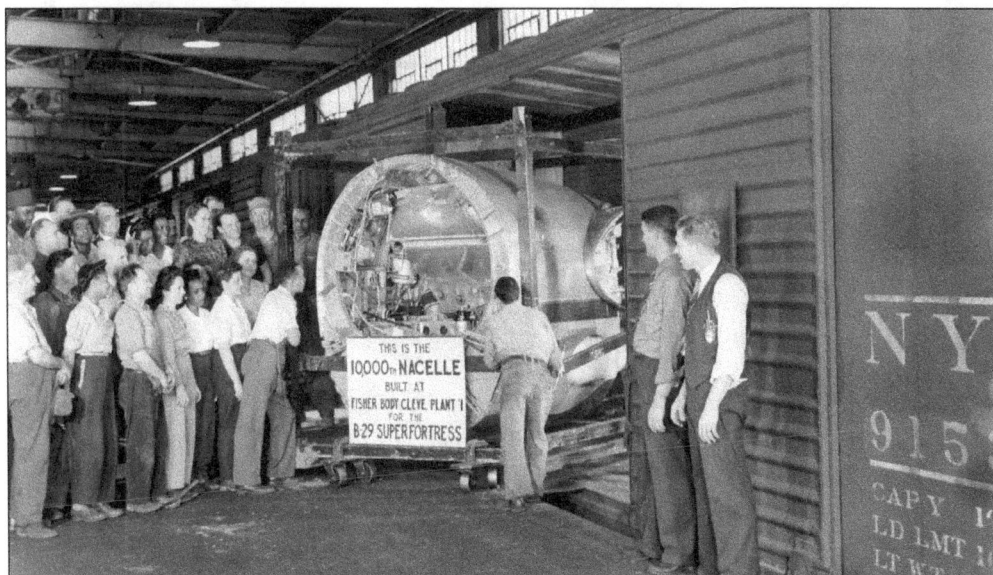

BUILDING NACELLES FOR THE B-29 BOMBERS. In March of 1945, wartime production continued. At the Fisher Body Plant, employees gathered to view their work—the 10,000th engine nacelle built for the B-29 Superfortress. At the height of war, the number of workers topped 14,000. Notice the number of women workers in the crowd, many of whom would continue working after the war had ended.

GREETINGS FROM HOME. Automotive, steel, and other heavy industries were not the only businesses to profit from the war. American Greetings Publishers, Inc., which became known as the American Greetings Corporation in the early 1950s, experienced its greatest sales in 1940. Here, at its west side plant on West 78th Street in Cleveland, two columns of female employees work an assembly line to prepare boxes of cards. (Photograph by James Thomas.)

AMERICAN SHIP BUILDING FOR WAR. Cleveland's natural setting along the Cuyahoga River and coast of Lake Erie made the shipbuilding industry profitable. During WWII, the American Ship Building Company, seen here beside the Cuyahoga River, provided many types of vessels for the war, including Liberty Ships and minesweepers. When many other businesses experienced postwar decline, American Ship Building grew to dominate the industry. (Photograph by John Nash.)

THE JACK & HEINZ COMPANY. Many industries in Cleveland excelled in wartime production, and the tremendous effort put forth by their employees was noted. Jack & Heinz, a company based in the inner-ring Cleveland suburb of Maple Heights, built airplane parts and following the war, was recognized by the War Department for outstanding production—the best put forth in the Greater Cleveland area. A sign in the shop reads, "You can't spell victory with an absence—keep up that work."

OTIS STEEL WORKS FOR WAR. Cleveland's abundant natural resources made it an ideal location for the creation of heavy industries, in particular, the steel industry. At one time, Cleveland was home to the giants of the steel market, including the Otis Steel Company, which during the height of WWII, was purchased by another steel titan, Jones & Laughlin Steel Corporation, based in Pittsburgh.

THE EAST OHIO GAS COMPANY EXPLOSION. Given the time this photograph was taken, it could have been of any theater of war in Europe. Instead, it was the scene of what was left of a machine shop razed by the gas explosion and fire that rocked the east side of Cleveland on October 20, 1944, around 3:00 p.m. Recovery and rescue efforts superceded the city's war effort as bodies were carried out on stretchers days after the devastation had occurred.

FIGHTING THE CONFLAGRATION. Members of the U.S. Coast Guard joined police, fire, and other Cleveland city workers to battle the flames engulfing 20 city blocks. Here, guardsmen fight flames at the house of Mary Hocevar on Lake Court with water pumped 1,400 feet from Lake Erie by Coast Guard fireboat. Leading the effort was Cleveland Fire Department's Captain John Denk, also chief of the Bureau of Fire Education.

THE GRIM TASK OF DIGGING FOR BODIES. Rescue workers and survivors sifted through the rubble and debris searching for bodies and hoping perhaps a survivor or two might still be found. The toll from the explosion and fire was unlike any disaster in Cleveland's history. An estimated $6 million worth of damage was sustained from the loss of 2 factories, 79 homes, over 200 cars, and the deaths of 130 residents and company workers.

THE COLLAPSED HOLDING TANK THAT STARTED THE FIRE. The East Ohio Gas Company fire and explosion resulted when a tank, pictured here, holding millions of gallons of liquid natural gas exploded. Flames shot high in the air at first, then spread to the surrounding residential area. While the exact cause of the explosion could never be determined, the end result would be the creation of safer means of storing natural gas.

"V" IS FOR VICTORY. On August 15, 1945, World War II ended in victory for the United States and her allies. One month prior, on July 4th, Clevelanders filled the lakefront Municipal Stadium to capacity for the annual Festival of Freedom celebration. Flags representing all nations were gathered in a "V" formation as victory drew near. Cleveland had done its part in mobilizing a gigantic effort to support the nation during wartime. (Photograph by Byron Filkins.)

MAYOR BURKE MEETS PRESIDENT TRUMAN. At the end of the war, Cleveland had a new mayor, Thomas A. Burke Jr., who is seen here shaking the hand of President Harry S. Truman, who led the nation to the conclusion of WWII. Mayor Burke served Cleveland through four consecutive terms. He first came to office when his predecessor, Mayor Lausche, became Ohio's governor in 1945. Burke Lakefront Airport was named in his honor. (Acme Newspictures.)

Three

POSTWAR PROGRESS

CLEVELAND MEMORIAL SHOREWAY. The Memorial Shoreway was the first east-west freeway in Cleveland and a precursor to the interstate highway system. Planned as a work-relief project, it was the largest Works Progress Administration (WPA) job in the country. Referred to as Shore Drive or Lakefront Road until World War II, it became the Memorial Shoreway in honor of the city's WWII veterans. This 1947 view was taken from the west end, near Clifton Boulevard and Lake Road. (Photograph by Glenn Zahn.)

AN ALL-AMERICAN CITY. In 1949, for the first time, Cleveland was named an All-American City. Cleveland's performance during the war helped maintain the city's image as a major player. As 1950 approached, Cleveland's population topped 910,000, its highest population yet. Seen here is the May Company, one of the city's leading retailers.

SAILING DOWN THE RIVER. The Terminal Tower rises in the background as a tugboat pulls a barge along the Cuyahoga River. The Baltimore & Ohio Railroad Jackknife Bridge, so named because when raised, it resembled a jackknife, allows the barge to pass. This photograph was taken from the old Superior Viaduct.

END OF AN ERA. John Wilmer Galbreath (right) shakes hands with Society for Savings President Mervin B. France, who cleared the way in 1950 for Galbreath to become the new Terminal Tower Group owner for the purchase price of $35,000,000. The negotiations were completed in a record 10 days. Realty partners Edgar L. Ostendorf and Warren Morris handled the transaction. Galbreath was no stranger to Cleveland. In 1944, he bought the consolidated plant of American Steel & Wire Company for $60,000. Galbreath, from Columbus, Ohio, was one of the biggest real estate owner / developers in the nation. The change in ownership was welcomed as an important and progressive move in the future development of Cleveland. The seller of the Terminal Tower Group was Robert R. Young, major stockholder of the interest. The Union Terminal was not part of the sale, as the New York Central and Nickel Plate Railroads owned it. In 1982, Forest City Enterprises purchased both the Terminal Tower and Union Station and renamed the new retail complex Tower City Center.

CLEVELAND'S NEWEST MAYOR. Anthony J. Celebrezze (left) takes the oath of office as mayor of Cleveland in November of 1953. Court of Appeals Judge Joy Seth Hurd swore him in at City Hall. As mayor from 1953 to 1962, Celebrezze guided Cleveland through a progressive post-war era that included an increase in industry and major urban renewal. Instead of seeking another term as mayor, Celebrezze left Cleveland to become the Secretary of Health and Education under the Kennedy Administration.

THE INNERBELT CONNECTION. The Innerbelt Freeway was the largest road-building project in Cleveland's history. Designed to move traffic around, rather than through, the downtown area, it was to link the Memorial Shoreway on the northeast with a new Medina Freeway extending out to Cleveland-Hopkins International Airport on the southwest. Shown here in 1959 is construction on the connecting interchange between the Innerbelt and the Shoreway, which later became known as "Deadman's Curve." (Photograph by Bernie Noble.)

The East 9th Street Pier. This is a 1951 aerial view of Cleveland's East 9th Street Pier. The East 9th Street Pier opened in 1913 when Cleveland's City Council leased property at the foot of East 9th Street for shipping use. The first ship to land on the new lake terminal was *The City of Buffalo*, arriving in 1915. In 1938, the Lederer Terminal Warehouse Company assumed the lease for the East 9th Street Pier. (Photograph by Robert Runyan.)

Opening of the St. Lawrence Seaway. On May 6, 1959, the first two-ocean going vessels entered the Cleveland harbor after passing through the newly opened St. Lawrence Seaway. At West 9th Street, Mayor Anthony Celebrezze (right) extends his hand as he and a civic committee greet Captain Otto Trautman of the 7,800-ton *Extavia*, the first American ship to arrive from overseas. That same day, the 8,000-ton *Byklefjell* docked at the Lederer Terminal at East 9th Street.

YEAR OF THE BIG SNOW. On Thanksgiving weekend in 1950, 30 inches of snow fell, paralyzing the City of Cleveland. Mayor Burke declared a state of emergency, and the Ohio National Guard was called to help clear the streets and to prevent widespread looting. Bulldozers and tanks were used to free cars and trucks from snow banks and snow drifts, which had accumulated in the middle of the streets. The scene here shows Euclid Avenue at East 77th Street.

THE BURNING RIVER. It was not a common occurrence for the Cuyahoga River to catch fire, but when it did, the image was nothing short of spectacular. In 1952, an oil slick on the river near Jefferson Avenue and West 3rd Street was ignited, causing smoke and flames to engulf the area. Fireboats were used to contain the conflagration, which resulted in damage totaling $1.5 million. (Photograph by James Thomas.)

THE TORNADO OF 1953. On June 8, 1953, around 9:45 p.m., a tornado struck the Cleveland area, ripping through the west side and leaving a trail of damage, debris, and death totaling $30 million. Here, friends and neighbors work on the home of Mrs. Jess Green on West 116th Street, which sustained heavy damage. It was one of 1,988 dwellings damaged, while another 50 were completely destroyed. In addition, 13 public school buildings were damaged by the high winds.

SURVIVORS DEAL WITH THE TORNADO'S AFTERMATH. The tornado that tore through Cleveland left 300 persons injured and 9 dead. The mayor called in the Ohio National Guard to help with the massive clean up operations and to prevent looting. Seen here are wind victims Wilma Jatzek, of the suburb of Seven Hills, pouring coffee for Mr. and Mrs. Felix Gorgone, as they sit in front of what was left of their home on Brooklawn Avenue.

DEDICATION OF THE WINDERMERE STATION. On March 15, 1955, the Cleveland Transit System, created in 1941, opened its new Windermere Rapid Transit station, thus inaugurating public rail transportation between Windermere and Public Square in downtown Cleveland.

THE DETROIT-WEST 98TH STREET RAPID TRANSIT STATION. Rapid transit service out to the West Park station began on August 14, 1955. Seen here is a westbound rapid transit car at the Detroit-West 98th Street Station on the first day of operations. In 1968, rapid transit service was extended to Cleveland-Hopkins International Airport, making Cleveland the first city in the nation to introduce rapid transit rail transportation between the downtown area and the airport.

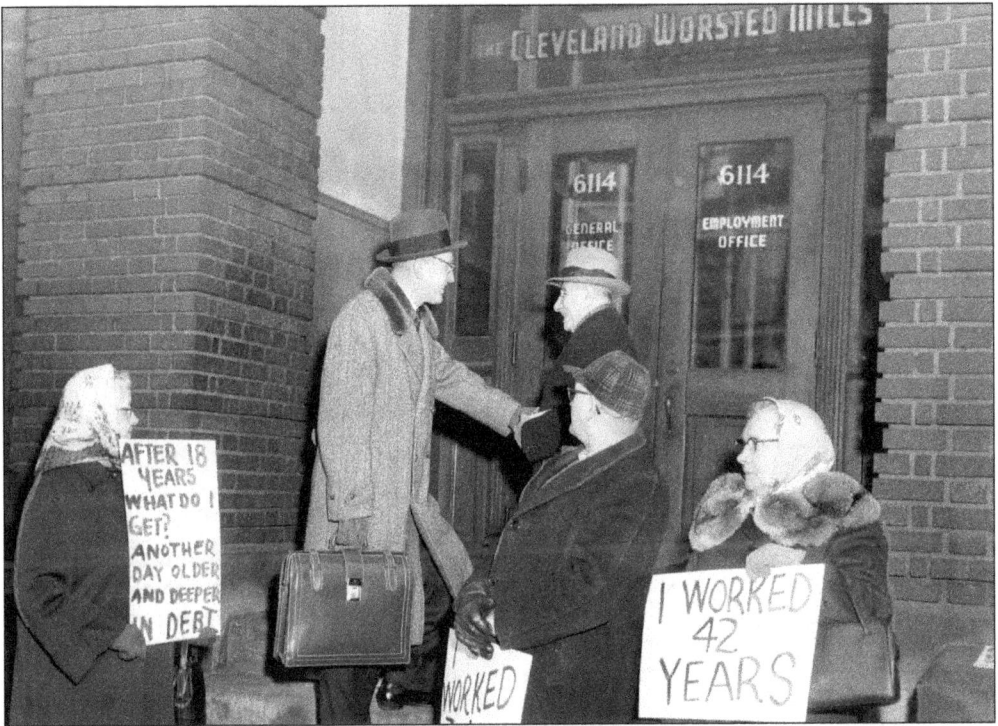

END OF THE CLEVELAND WORSTED MILLS. Post-WWII recovery was not realized by some businesses and industries in Cleveland. In January of 1956, senior picketers plead against the liquidation of the Cleveland Worsted Mills Company in the neighborhood of Fleet and Broadway. Holding signs indicating how many years of their lives they had invested in the company, they are (left to right) Mrs. Mary Kinderfinski, Charles Gorman, and Mrs. Sophie Szelinski. At the door is union attorney Howard Metzenbaum (with briefcase) confronting stockholder Charles Goldsmith.

THE FISHER BODY PLANT. The automotive industry did well after the war. The Fisher Body Plant at East 140th Street and Coit Road started building cars in 1921. Five years later, it became a division of General Motors. During World War II, the plant produced tank and gun parts and engine nacelles for the B-29 aircraft. Here, an aerial view shows the new five-acre parking lot built in 1960 to accommodate employment growth. The plant closed in 1983.

GROUNDBREAKING FOR URBAN RENEWAL. Erieview was the name given to the ambitious urban renewal project begun in the early 1960s to remove blight from the area northeast of the immediate downtown Cleveland area. Here, a crowd of approximately 200 gathers to witness the ceremonies for the first demolition, done by the Harris Wrecking Company, which would officially start the renovation. Erieview came right after the opening of the new 21-story East Ohio Gas Building on East 9th Street and Superior Avenue.

ERIEVIEW BEGINS TO TAKE SHAPE. In May of 1964, Erieview Tower was completed and became the cornerstone of the urban renewal project that encompassed East 6th through East 17th Streets and continued from Chester Avenue to Lake Erie. Standing before the tower are (left to right) architect Jack Hayes, Director of Urban Renewal James Lester, and I.M. Pei, the planner and genius behind Erieview. (Photograph by Tony Tomsic.)

ERIEVIEW TOWER. When Erieview Tower was completed, it stood 40 stories high as it anchored East 12th Street and St. Clair Avenue. At the time, it was the second tallest office building in Ohio. Architect I.M. Pei used the more modern International style in his design. Several additional buildings would be completed as part of the Erieview project, including a new Federal Building, the Public Utilities Building, and the Bond Court office building.

ERIEVIEW PLAZA. While attracting business to the downtown area was the impetus behind Erieview's bold design, planners were also mindful of drawing visitors to the area who might otherwise not venture to downtown Cleveland. A plaza and reflecting pool spanning three blocks was incorporated into the design. In the wintertime, the pool would freeze and attract a crowd of enthusiastic ice skaters. (Photograph by Clayton Knipper.)

49

THE NEW SHERATON-CLEVELAND HOTEL. When multimillionaire real estate developer John Galbreath purchased the Terminal Tower Group, he acquired his first hotel, the Hotel Cleveland. In 1959, major national hotel chain Sheraton moved in to establish Sheraton-Cleveland as an anchor of the Terminal Tower. While the hotel business did not experience the kind of expansion seen in other industries, Cleveland was still a viable location for conventions, making the Sheraton chain a welcome addition.

DOWNTOWN FESTIVAL DAYS. As Cleveland prepared to enter the 1960s, there was much to celebrate. The Innerbelt Freeway opened, major urban renewal was underway with Erieview, industrial expansion set new records, and a new 22-story Electric Illuminating Building was completed on Public Square. In May of 1961, Mayor Celebrezze addressed a crowd downtown during the festival days, when Cleveland had an opportunity to display its finest through food and fun. (Photograph by Herman Seid.)

Four

CLEVELAND CHANGES

CLEVELAND: NOW! In May of 1968, a patch of grass on Public Square in front of the Terminal Tower was elaborately landscaped to draw attention to the Cleveland: NOW! urban renewal program endorsed by Mayor Carl B. Stokes. Like many major American cities during the 1960s and 1970s, Cleveland experienced problems including school segregation, racial tension, urban blight, unemployment, and population decline. The Cleveland: Now! program addressed these concerns. (Photograph by Tony Tomsic.)

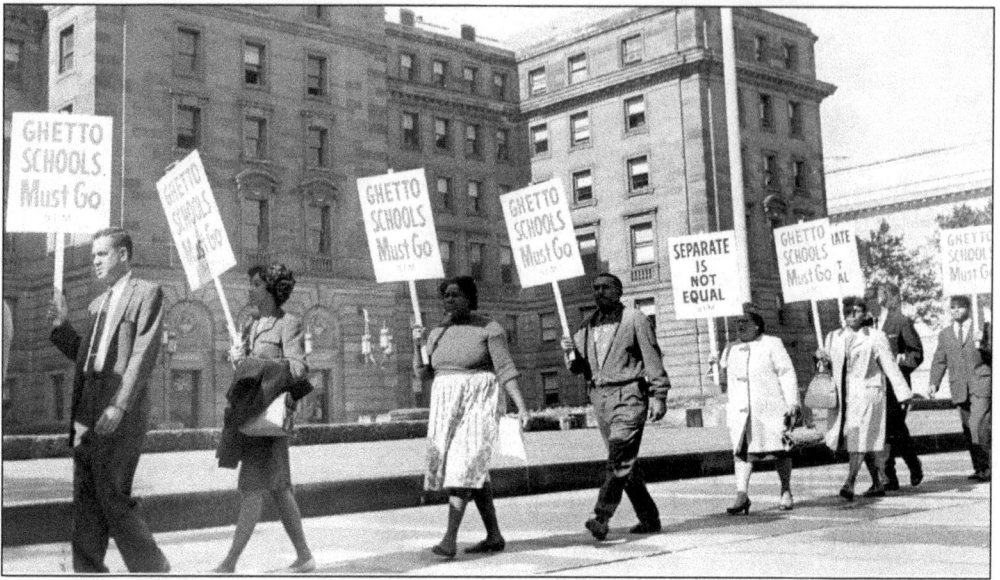

GHETTO SCHOOLS MUST GO! During the early 1960s, Cleveland public schools had an unprecedented student population nearing 135,000. To accommodate the large student base, programs were adopted to ease overcrowding. These usually included half-days and remedial programs, which typically undercut African-American students' educations. At the start of the school year in September of 1963, protestors organized by the NAACP picketed against Cleveland's segregated school system in front of the Board of Education.

SIT-IN FOR DESEGREGATION. One of the protests led by Civil Rights leaders to end segregation involved busing African-American students from crowded, run-down schools on the east side to predominately white schools on the west side that were not as crowded and in much better condition. Here, in 1964, protestors bar entrance to the office of Memorial School in Little Italy in an effort to end segregation. (Photograph by Bernie Noble.)

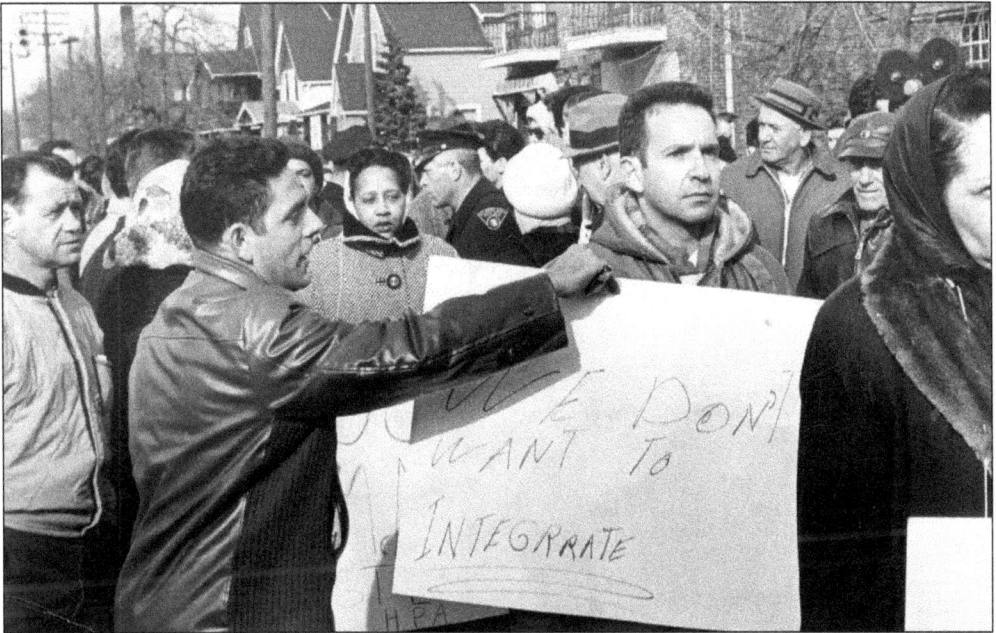

WE DON'T WANT TO INTEGRATE! Little Italy, a largely Italian-American neighborhood on Murray Hill and Mayfield Road on Cleveland's east side, did not want African-American students integrated into the Murray Hill School District. Instead, they preferred the construction of new schools, which civil rights leaders pointed out only perpetuated segregation. Here, in 1964, protestors march in front of Memorial School to voice their discontent. (Photograph by Bernie Noble.)

FUROR OVER INTEGRATION. Tension continued to mount in 1964 as residents of Little Italy clashed with opponents of segregation. At its worst, the violence led to many injuries and even death. Here, a fight broke out in front of a market on Murray Hill after protestors had picketed City Hall earlier, holding placards that read, "Remember, this is Big America, not Little Italy." Fortunately, no serious injuries resulted from this confrontation.

MAYOR LOCHER TOURS HOUGH. Mayor Ralph Locher (center) wore a solemn expression as he toured the riot-torn Hough neighborhood on July 19, 1966, one day after the Hough Riots had begun. Scattered violence brought on by racial tensions erupted in the neighborhood, which extended from East 55th to East 105th Streets. On the night of July 18th, one woman was killed and 15 people were injured in the melee. (United Press International photograph.)

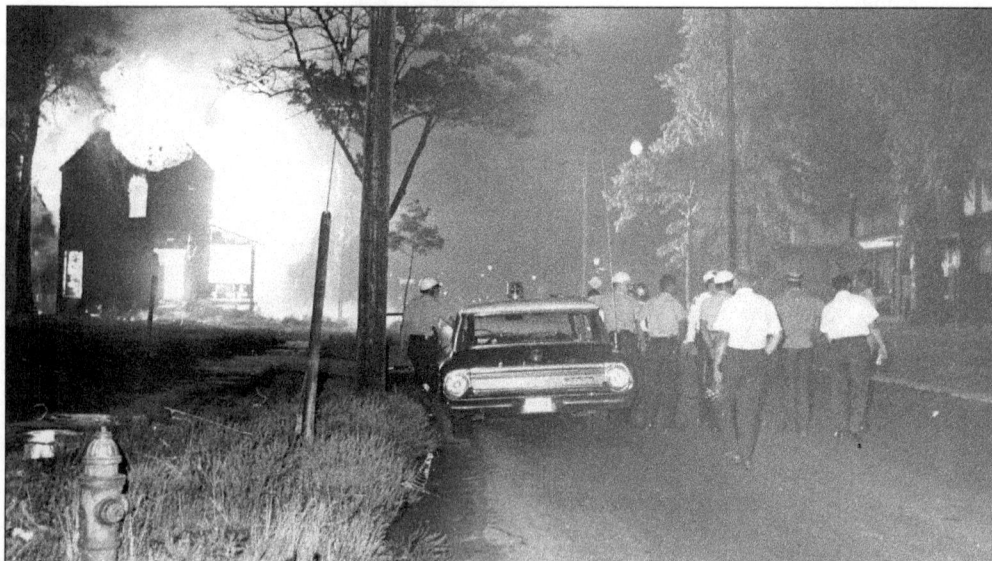

HOUGH NEIGHBORHOOD AFLAME. The Hough Riots lasted approximately one week, from July 18th to July 24th, 1966. The administration of Mayor Locher was defined by the riots, which erupted in part because of his support of a segregated school system and his perceived ineffectiveness in bridging the increasing racial divide. Here, Cleveland police trying to curtail rioters invade the area between East 86th Street and Linwood Avenue. (Photograph by Herman Seid.)

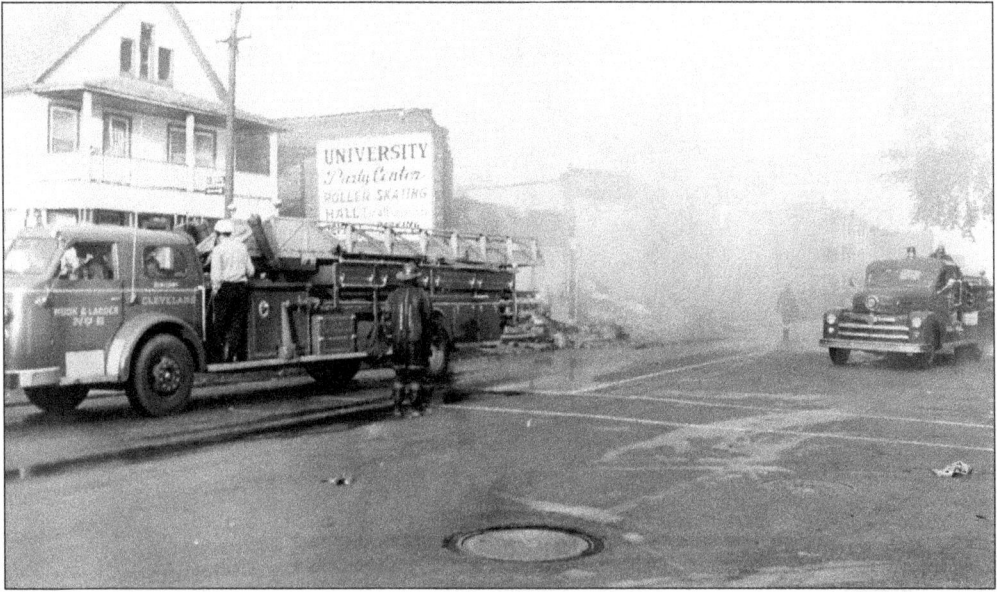

THE HOUGH RIOTS BY DAY. The rioting in Cleveland's Hough neighborhood drew national and international attention. In this photograph, Cleveland firefighters on 24-hour riot duty prepare to battle yet another arson committed on residential and commercial property. The University Party Center and Roller Skating Hall was the target of an alleged firebomb. (Photograph by Herman Seid.)

LOCHER CALLS THE NATIONAL GUARD. Two days into the riots on July 20th, Mayor Locher called for help from the National Guard to restore peace in the neighborhood. The area was all but closed down to prevent random outbursts of violence. Here, on July 25th, National Guardsmen stand watch at East 79th Street and Hough Avenue, near the 79er's Café. Locher's diminished credibility in the African-American community cost him the mayorship. (Photograph by Frank Aleksandrowicz.)

MAYOR CARL B. STOKES. In November of 1967, Carl B. Stokes took the oath of office as the first African-American mayor of a major American city. He won the support not only of members of the African-American community but of many in the white community who tired of the racial polarization that plagued the city. Here, Democrat Mayor Stokes is at Audubon Jr. High School in May of 1968 to raise support for his ambitious urban renewal program, Cleveland: NOW! (Photograph by Van Dillard.)

BROTHERS CARL AND LOUIS STOKES. Carl (left) and Louis Stokes were brothers and law partners, as well as the most influential set of politicians in Cleveland, particularly during the city's tumultuous period. As native Clevelanders, they each sought to leave their imprint on a city in need of new direction and rehabilitation. Carl Stokes made history and achieved national and international acclaim as Cleveland's mayor. Louis Stokes became an influential Democratic congressman in Washington, D.C.

MAYOR STOKES VISITS EDGEWATER POOL. Mayor Stokes paused to be interviewed as he was surrounded by a group of very enthusiastic children on the day he and Utilities Director Ben S. Stefanski (to the right of Stokes) helped dedicate the new Edgewater Pool. The opening took place on July 4, 1969, the day of the big storm, which struck northeast Ohio later in the afternoon, putting an abrupt end to the 4th of July festivities. (Photograph by John W. Mott.)

THE INFAMOUS FIRE ON CUYAHOGA RIVER. Mayor Stokes stands in the center of this photograph talking to a woman as he holds a press conference on a railroad bridge that was burned when an oil slick caught fire on the Cuyahoga River. This particular fire, which occurred on June 22, 1969, received national press and left Cleveland the butt of many bad jokes. After all, how many cities would want the dubious honor of having had a burning river? (Photograph by Herman Seid.)

THE GLENVILLE RIOTS. Also referred to as the "Glenville Shootout," the Glenville Riots were the first crises of the mayoral administration of Carl B. Stokes. Unlike the random events that hand unfolded in the Hough neighborhood leading to violence, the Glenville riots could be traced to a militant named Fred "Ahmed" Evans, who on July 23, 1968, exchanged gunfire with Cleveland police over an alleged sale of illegal weapons. Four persons were killed the first night. (Photograph by Ron Kuntz.)

BY ORDER OF THE MAYOR, BLACKS ONLY! As the rioting continued on July 24th in the Superior-Lakeview section of Glenville, Mayor Stokes took the bold step of asking that all white persons, including the police, stay out of the neighborhood until order could be restored. Racial tensions ran so deep that Stokes believed, and rightly so, that only a black presence could secure the peace. In fact, the *Cleveland Press* photographer who took this image, Van Dillard, was African American.

THE NATIONAL GUARD ENTERS GLENVILLE. On July 25, 1968, the National Guard was called to Glenville as it had been during the Hough Riots. By this time, however, the violence was confined to random arson and theft. Here, the Reverend DeForrest Brown (in center) greets the arriving guardsmen at East 195th and Superior Avenue. (Photograph by Van Dillard.)

PEACE IS RESTORED IN GLENVILLE. Five days after the first gunshots were exchanged, peace came to Glenville. When the final cost of the violence was tallied, over 60 businesses, many of which were neighborhood stores, were ruined for a total loss to the neighborhood of Glenville of over $2.5 million. Another casualty of the riot was Mayor Stokes' short-lived Cleveland: NOW! program. When it was discovered that Fred Evans had received money from the project, contributions ended. (Photograph by Ted Schneider.)

CLEVELAND'S SUPER SESQUI! On July 23, 1971, a crowd of admirers on Public Square surrounded Mayor Stokes as he prepared to cut the city's birthday cake in celebration of the sesquicentennial, or the 175th anniversary, of the founding of the City. Radio station WGCL was one of many sponsors of the festivities, which drew thousands to Public Square. Cleveland had undergone many changes, some more dramatic than others. The Hough Riots and the Glenville Shootout highlighted racial tensions, but also left opportunity for the city to work together toward peaceful solutions: the Northeast Ohio Areawide Coordinating Agency was formed to regulate the use of federal funds for big-city needs, and the Cleveland American Indian Center was formed to address the concerns of Native Americans. Carl B. Stokes served two terms as mayor of Cleveland, from 1967 to 1971, after which he moved to New York where he pursued a broadcasting career. He returned to Cleveland in 1980 to resume his legal career. Carl Stokes passed away in 1996. (Photograph by Van Dillard.)

NATIVE AMERICAN CONFRONTATION. An unexpected peace talk was forced upon dignitaries of the Sesquicentennial Commission: (left to right) Louis B. Seltzer, commission chairman and longtime editor of *The Cleveland Press*; Russell Means of the Cleveland American Indian Movement; Clay Herrick (as Moses Cleaveland); and Dennis Bowens, met to discuss the concerns of Native Americans. (Photograph by Tom Prusha.)

MOSES CLEAVELAND LANDED HERE! Cleveland's "Super Sesqui" celebration was seized as an opportunity by Native Americans to draw attention to their cause. At the celebration, they confronted members of the Sesqui Centennial Commission at the foot of West Superior Avenue on the Cuyahoga River. A crowd that had disembarked the Goodtime II cruise ship and demonstrators gathered at the site where Moses Cleaveland first landed to witness the event. (Photograph by Tom Prusha.)

MAYOR RALPH J. PERK. Ralph Perk succeeded Carl Stokes as mayor, serving three terms until 1977. In this photograph, Mayor Perk is given the oath of office in November of 1971 at Cleveland City Hall in a ceremony attended by (left to right) Mrs. Helen Kucinich, Councilman Dennis Kucinich, Ricky Perk, Detective James McHugh (above Ricky's head), Mayor Ralph Perk, Mrs. Perk, and attorney Franklin A. Polk.

PASSING THE TORCH. Outgoing Mayor Carl B. Stokes (right) who decided against seeking a third term, congratulates his successor, Mayor Ralph J. Perk (left), a Republican. Unlike his immediate predecessors, Mayor Perk would not face any major hostilities in the city, but would have to face the beginnings of Cleveland's major financial problems. Perk succeeded in securing government grants for city improvements, but these would prove to be too costly for his administration to handle successfully. (Photograph by Tony Tomsic.)

COUNCILMAN DENNIS KUCINICH. Dennis Kucinich (left) began his lengthy political career as Ward 7 councilman on Cleveland's west side. Kucinich, a Democrat, quickly gained a reputation for outspokenness and straight-talk, which attracted national attention. Here, councilman Kucinich gives his views on big-city problems to reporter Carolyn Lewis (right) as producer Chris Gaul (center) looks on. Lewis and Gaul were visiting Cleveland to gather material for a PBS special, *The Cities: Uncle Sam, Can You Spare A Dime*, which explored how big cities sought solutions to their varied problems. (Photograph by Jenkins Scott / WVIZ.)

MAYOR DENNIS KUCINICH. Dennis Kucinich only served one term as mayor from 1977 to 1979, but it was a memorable one, as he was the youngest elected mayor of a major American city. Here, he is administered the oath of office by Ohio Supreme Court Justice Ralph Locher, former mayor of Cleveland. Mayor Kucinich's wife, Sandy, stands by his side. Since 1975, Kucinich had held the post of clerk of Cleveland Municipal Court.

THE MAYOR AND THE COUNCIL PRESIDENT. George Forbes (left) was the longtime Cleveland City Council president, beginning in 1973 under the administration of Mayor Ralph Perk and continuing his run alongside Mayor Dennis Kucinich. Forbes wielded considerable influence and had a reputation for outspokenness and aggressiveness, which made him one of the most controversial council leaders in recent history.

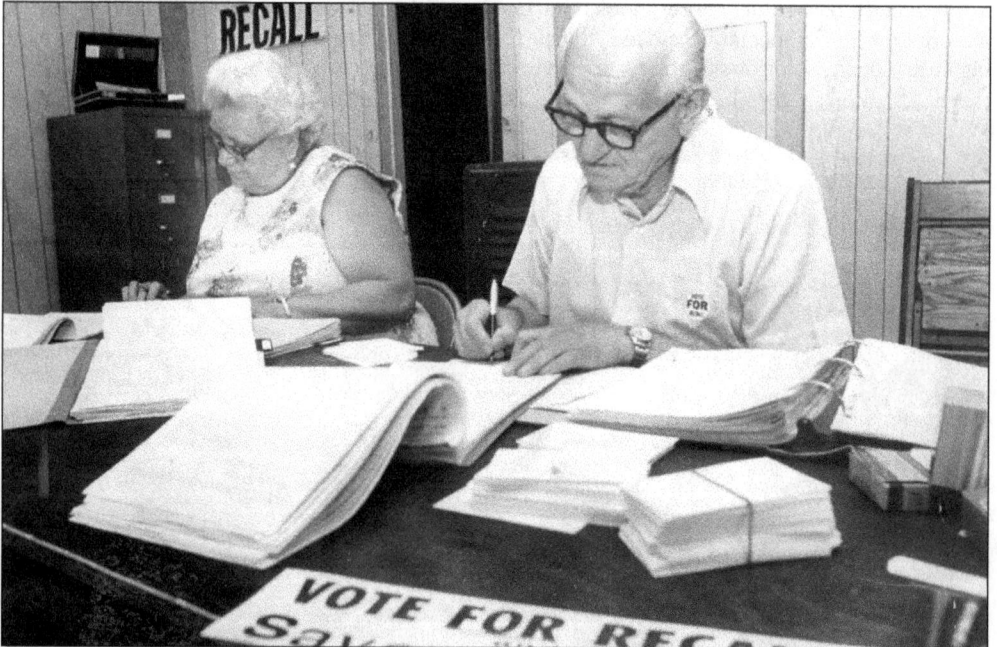

THE RECALL ELECTION OF 1978. Mayor Kucinich's confrontational style in politics often offended not only his rivals, but also his grass-roots supporters. Many believed the mayor reached an all-time low when he fired the popular police chief, Richard Hongisto. A movement took hold to oust Cleveland's mayor. Recall volunteers Mary Dietrich (left) and Tony Abella (right) check recall petitions. (Photograph by Tim Culek.)

MAYOR KUCINICH CASTS HIS VOTE.
Dennis Kucinich once again made
Cleveland history by becoming the first
mayor ever to face a recall election. The
required number of petitions had been
gathered to force Kucinich from office.
When Mayor Kucinich refused to resign,
a vote was called for, and on August 13,
1978, he won the fight to stay in office by
a mere 236 votes, even after two recounts.
Kucinich opponents had their say in the
next election when he failed in his bid for a
second term as Cleveland's mayor.

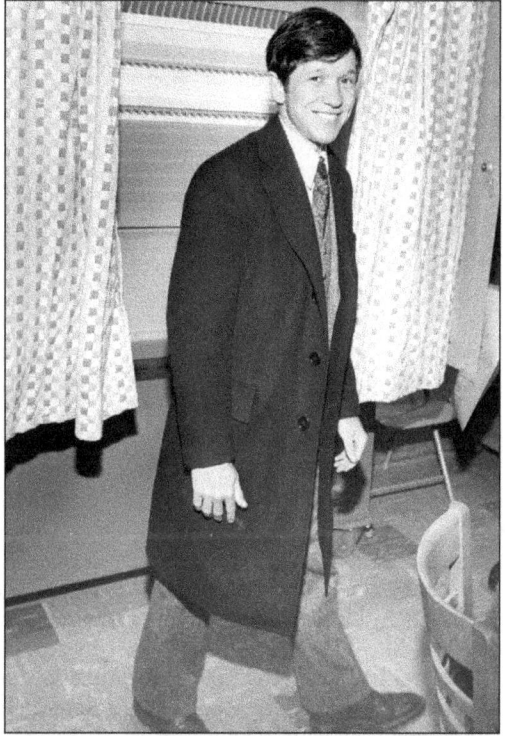

DEFAULT COUNCIL. The administration of Mayor Kucinich will perhaps best be remembered
for being at the helm when Cleveland fell into default, marking the first time since the Great
Depression that any major American city had faced such financial ruin. When Mayor Kucinich
resisted attempts by the Cleveland Electric Illuminating Company to purchase city-owned
Municipal, or Muny, Light and thus to monopolize Cleveland's power supply, local banks
supportive of CEI called in their loans.

MAYOR GEORGE V. VOINOVICH. In 1979, Republican George Voinovich defeated Mayor Kucinich and inherited a city in financial trouble. At this press conference held in November of 1980, Mayor Voinovich highlighted Cleveland's misspent bond funds and announced that Cleveland had, with the help of local banks, come out of default. Next to Mayor Voinovich is longtime Council Clerk Mercedes Cotner and beside her, city Finance Director William Reidy. (Photograph by Paul Toppelstein.)

VOINOVICH AND OAKAR. During the administration of Mayor Voinovich, Cleveland City Council introduced significant changes to the office of mayor and for the members of City Council—changes not seen since Cleveland was under the city manager plan. In 1981, the terms for mayor and council member were doubled from two to four years, and the number of council members was reduced from 33 to 21. Here, Voinovich chats with supporter and west side councilwoman Mary Rose Oakar. (Photograph by Van Dillard.)

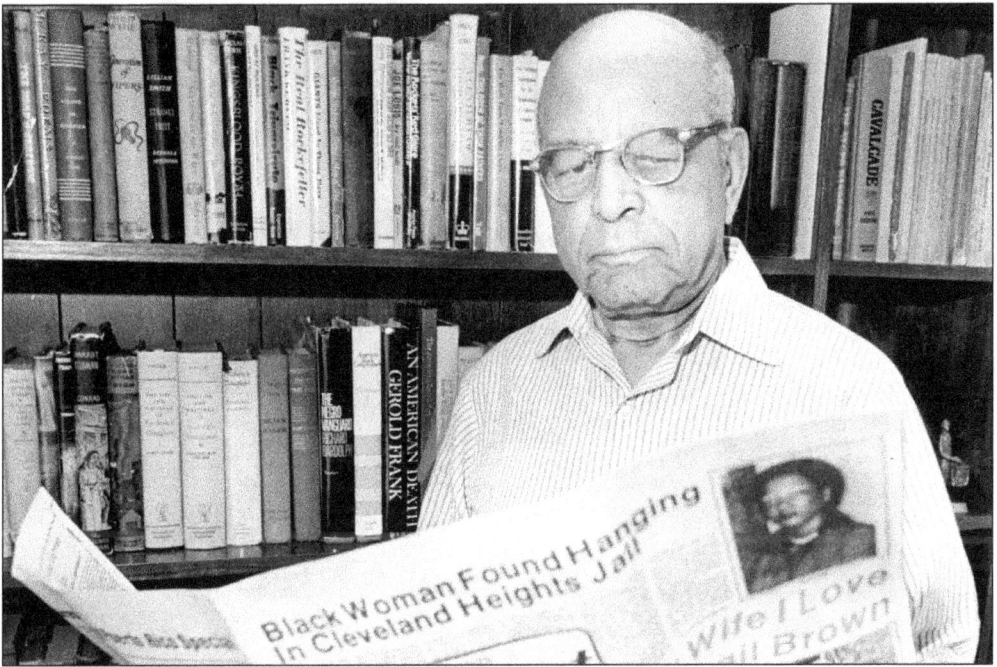

WILLIAM O. WALKER. Here, William Otis Walker (1896–1981) holds a copy of his publication, *The Call and Post*, which he began managing in 1932. He eventually rose to become majority owner and editor. Originally from Selma, Alabama, Walker distinguished himself in politics as a conservative Republican. He supported the Civil Rights Movement and backed Carl Stokes when he sought to become mayor. Walker was the first African American to hold a cabinet-level position in Ohio. (Photograph by Larry Nighswander.)

AN INFLUENTIAL TRIO. Seated left to right in 1978 are Michael White, Arnold Pinkney, and William O. Walker, three of the most recognizable leaders in the Cleveland community. Michael White would succeed George Voinovich as mayor, becoming only the second African American to hold Cleveland's highest office. Businessman Arnold Pinkney was president of the Cleveland School Board during desegregation, and W.O. Walker had the black community's ear as editor of *The Call and Post*. (Photograph by Van Dillard.)

COUNCIL MEMBER FANNIE LEWIS. Longtime City Council member Fannie Lewis, representing the Hough community in 1982, handed over petitions signed by over 40 Hough residents to Michael Diercouff of Housing and Urban Development (HUD). Lewis had a reputation for fiercely defending the rights and concerns of her community and was one of the council's most outspoken members. She remains an active member of City Council, focusing on jobs for Clevelanders.

OPPOSING POINTS OF VIEW. Roldo Bartimole, founder of the independent *Point of View* newspaper in Cleveland, was forcibly thrown out of a Cleveland City Council meeting in 1981 by the council president himself, George Forbes, after Bartimole refused to leave the closed-door City Council meeting. George Forbes was not a stranger to controversy. (Photograph by Tim Culek.)

LONNIE L. BURTEN JR. Cleveland City Councilman and social activist Lonnie Burten represented Ward 12, encompassing the Central-Woodland neighborhood, from 1975 until his murder in 1984 at the age of 40. Burten did not support public housing, opening instead the Central Area Development Corporation to promote private home ownership. Here, Burten surveys one of the projects in his ward. He would spend his own money and give his own time to help low-income residents live in decent homes.

BURTEN CHALLENGES FORBES. Lonnie Burten's unwavering support of the impoverished often placed him in direct confrontation with City Council President George Forbes. In 1981, Burten (at the podium) announced his intentions to unseat Forbes as council leader. Those present at the occasion were: (left to right) John Lynch, Jay Westbrook, Gary Kucinich, John Zayne, Michael Polensek, Burten, Dale Miller, Jim Rokakis, Tyrone Bolden, Edmund Ciolek, and Larry Jones. Burten won the support of 10 of his colleagues. (Photograph by Tim Culek.)

BATTISTI FAVORS BUSING.
Clevelanders cannot mention busing without naming the federal judge who ordered the desegregation of public schools: Frank J. Battisti (1922–1994). As a member of the U.S. District Court for the Northern District of Ohio, Judge Battisti decided in the 1976 court case *Reed v. Rhodes* that the answer to Cleveland's segregated school system was not to build more schools, but to integrate east and west side students into the same classrooms. (Photograph by Bernie Noble.)

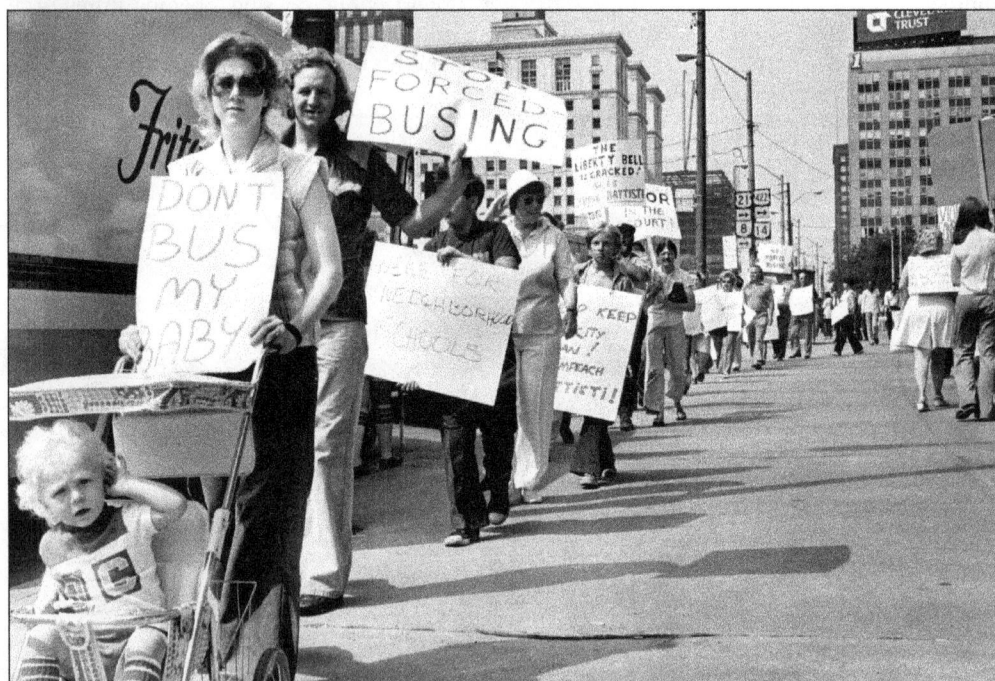

DON'T BUS MY BABY! Hailed by many as long overdue, Judge Battisti's landmark decision was not enthusiastically welcomed by parents who were forced to abandon their neighborhood schools and send their children across the river. The predominately white west side reacted negatively, forcing many to protest the ruling. Those who could afford to simply moved to the surrounding suburbs. (Photograph by Frank Reed.)

TAKING THE BUS TO SCHOOL. In September of 1979, security aide Lyda Carper (with notepad) checked the names of students as they prepared to board Cleveland school bus No. 426 as it headed for Oliver Hazard Perry School. Many parents accompanied their children to the bus stops, as students traveled across town often for the first time. At its height, busing moved nearly 35,000 students using 600 public school buses and other vehicles. (Photograph by Tim Culek.)

MAKING THE TRIP TO THE EAST SIDE. In October of 1980, students from the west side boarded a Cleveland school bus stopped at West 98th Street and Loretta Avenue, an average lower-middle class neighborhood of duplexes, for their daily commute to school on the east side of town. As desegregation entered phase three, the across-town rides became routine. (Photograph by Bernie Noble.)

CHILDREN COMING TOGETHER. By the time school desegregation entered the final stage, tensions had lessened, and students learned to get along. In September of 1980, students at Kenneth W. Clement School enjoyed the outdoors and each other during their back-to-school celebration. For a short time, busing solved the problem of segregation in public schools, but lack of adequate funding and public support would in the long run further erode Cleveland schools. (Photograph by Paul Toppelstein.)

RIDING THE RTA TO SCHOOL. In 1974, the Greater Cleveland Regional Transit Authority, or RTA, replaced the old Cleveland Transit System. Here, one of the new buses (on the left) delivered to the new RTA passes by the Soldiers and Sailors Monument on Public Square. Budget cuts forced the city to put some school children on public transportation. At the time, no one imagined that these buses would replace the yellow school bus in taking Cleveland public students to school. (Photograph by Paul Toppelstein.)

Five

CULTURAL HIGHLIGHTS

THE GREATER CLEVELAND HOME AND FLOWER SHOW. An annual winter event in Northeast Ohio since 1941, the Home and Flower Show is seen here in March of 1959 at its original location in Public Hall in downtown Cleveland. The show drew thousands of visitors who came to see the latest in home improvements and to admire the spectacular gardens and floral displays. The show is now held at the International Exposition Center (I-X) near Cleveland-Hopkins Airport. (Photograph by Byron Filkins.)

THE CLEVELAND CULTURAL GARDENS. The idea of recognizing Cleveland's ethnic diversity using cultural gardens was conceived in 1925 by newspaper editor Leo Weidenthal. He organized the Cleveland Cultural Gardens Federation to supervise the development of gardens and statuary representative of every ethnic group. Seen here is the main entrance to the gardens, north of Superior Avenue, as it appeared in 1972. (Photograph by Timothy Culek.)

THE GREEK CULTURAL GARDENS. On June 8, 1940, the royal Greek minister to Washington, D.C., Kimon Diamantopoulos, cut the ceremonial ribbon to officially open the Greek Cultural Gardens as Cleveland Mayor Harold H. Burton looked on. The Greek Cultural Gardens were one of dozens lining Liberty Boulevard (now Martin Luther King Jr. Boulevard) and East Boulevard in Cleveland. (Photograph by James Thomas.)

EASTERN ORTHODOX FESTIVAL OF NATIONALITIES. There were many ethnic dancers in Cleveland, and in the summer of 1961, the Eastern Orthodox Festival of Nationalities featured the Greek dance the "tsamiko," performed by Mrs. Anne Pager (center). She was joined by dancers representing different nationalities in their ethnic costumes: (left to right) John Hategan, Romanian; Donna Hallick, Ukrainian; Lila Kalinich, Serbian; Olga Michalczyk, White Russian; Virginia Tasi, Albanian; Minnie Darwish, Syrian; Sandra Mindala, Russian; and Peter Katelanos, Greek.

THE CLEVELAND BALLET. Cleveland was once home to the internationally acclaimed Cleveland Ballet Company founded in 1976 by dancers Dennis Nahat and Ian Horvath. Horvath is seen here lifting dancer Cynthia Graham into the air during a 1980 performance of a Cleveland holiday favorite, *The Nutcracker*. When not on tour, the Cleveland Ballet performed at the State Theater in Playhouse Square. (Photograph by Tim Culek.)

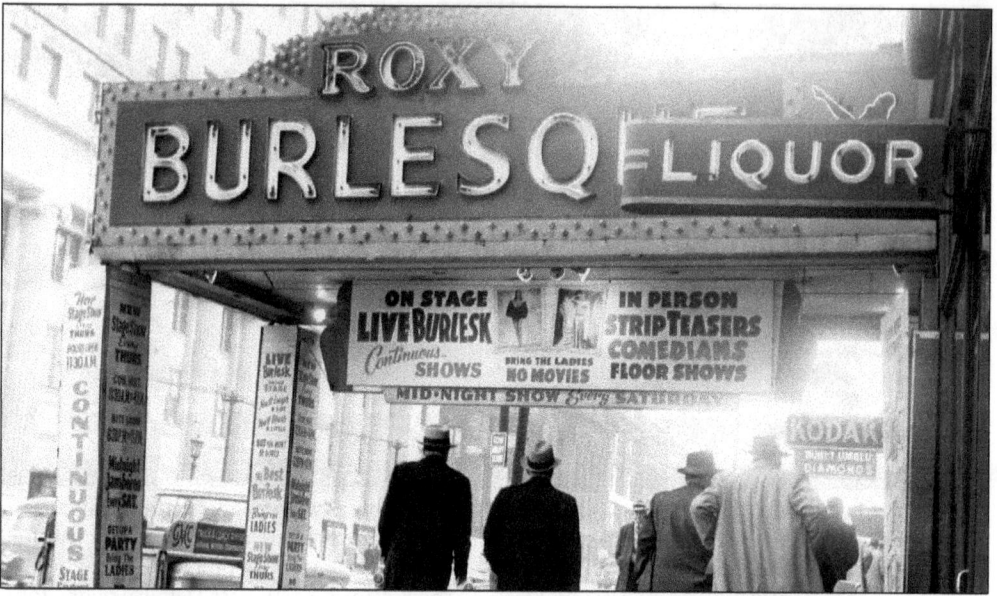

THE ROXY THEATER. Cleveland has always catered to a variety of interests, burlesque being no exception. Seen here in 1956, the Roxy Theater was Cleveland's premiere house of burlesque and even had a national reputation for excellence, which made it a major stop for the best acts in the business, like Blaze Starr, and featured legendary performers such as Abbott & Costello. The Roxy deteriorated over time and became an X-rated theater. It was eventually purchased by National City Bank and razed.

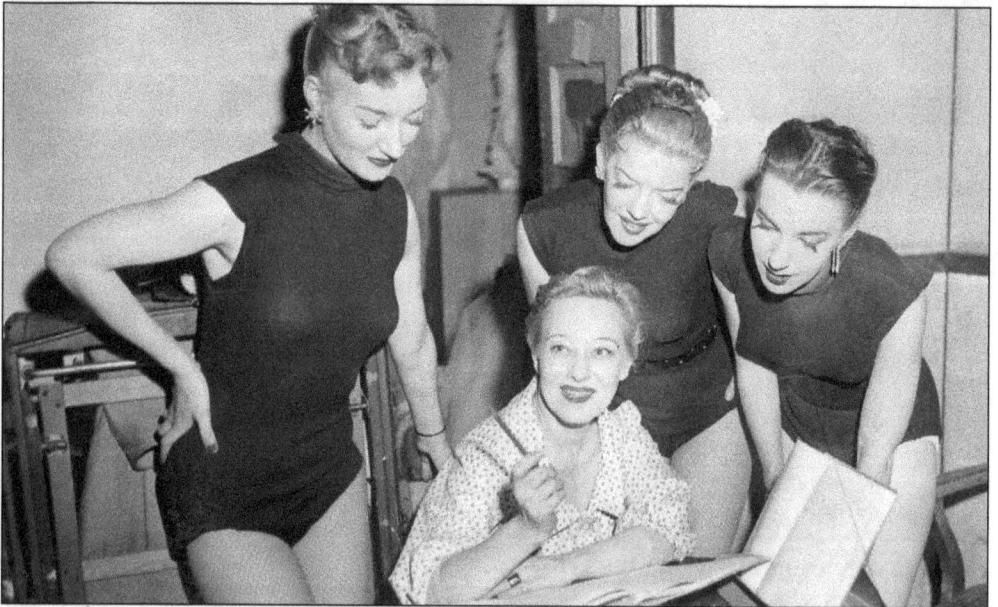

BOOKS AND BURLESQUE. In this photograph taken in May of 1957 backstage at the Roxy Theater, Cleveland's famed house of burlesque, fan dancer and crowd favorite Sally Rand (seated at table) studies for her college science and psychology courses in hopes of pursuing a change in profession. Rand is sharing her knowledge with fellow dancers (left to right) Roxy Lynn, Madeline Mixon, and Gaby Gerard. (Photograph by John Nash.)

76

"SHORT VINCENT." From the late 1920s through the 1950s, Vincent Street was the center of downtown Cleveland's nightlife, with high-quality dining, gambling, and big-name jazz entertainment drawing many visitors. Although popular, the street was often the target of civic outrage and police crack-down operations. The home of such downtown landmarks at the Theatrical, Kornman's Restaurant, the Grogshop, the Taystee Barbeque, and Frank Ciccia's Barbershop, it was the gathering place of gamblers, bookies, racketeers, lawyers, newspapermen, and sports figures.

TOMMY DORSEY AT THE PALACE THEATER. A crowd of more than 500 swing music fans crowded the Palace Theater stage in April 1928 to hear Tommy Dorsey and his Orchestra. Here, bandleader Tommy Dorsey is standing while playing the trombone. After the last act, theater management cleared the stage and invited the audience to dance if they wished or to just sit back and enjoy the music and keep time by stamping their feet.

KARAMU HOUSE. Karamu Director Olcutt Sanders and his assistant, Evelyn Phillips, admire the new Karamu House sign presented in 1964 by the Golden Agers club in honor of Russell and Rowena Jelliffe who had founded Karamu nearly 50 years earlier as a cultural arts center serving the African-American community. Karamu House is located on East 89th Street and Quincy Avenue. (Photograph by Glenn Zahn.)

THE KARAMU DANCERS. In 1959, the Karamu House Dancers took part in a production called *Jamaica*. Karamu House distinguished itself as an outstanding amateur theater and showcased many up and coming artists who otherwise may not have had an opportunity to perform. Karamu House offered classes in theater, dance, voice, and visual arts for neighborhood youth desiring to pursue a career in the arts.

THE CLEVELAND PLAY HOUSE. The Cleveland Play House, seen here in 1971, was located on East 77th Street and Euclid Avenue. It was Cleveland's premier theater company and one of the oldest in the country. The Play House included a large main theater and several smaller stages, seating anywhere from 150 to over 500 patrons. It was both an entertainment and an educational theater. In 1983, this theater was replaced with a more modern facility on East 85th and Euclid. (Photograph by Van Dillard.)

MARGARET HAMILTON. Native Clevelander Margaret Hamilton (1902–1985) is best remembered as the Wicked Witch of the West in *The Wizard of Oz*. Before she assumed this role, Hamilton appeared on stage at the Play House. She returned frequently to the Cleveland stage, as she did here in 1978 where she played Mrs. Bramson in *Night Must Fall* in the Drury Theater at the Play House. Reading to her character is Mary Adams-Smith, as her niece, Olivia.

THE CLEVELAND INSTITUTE OF ART. Pictured here in 1958 is the new Cleveland Institute of Art building located on East Boulevard and Bellflower Road in University Circle. It was designed in the International style and houses classrooms, studios, galleries, an auditorium, and a library. Students can choose from a variety of art specialties as they work to attain their Bachelor of Fine Arts (BFA) degree from the art institute. (Photograph by Frank Aleksandrowicz.)

HOME OF SUPERMAN. In 1933, two Glenville High Schools students created Superman, one of the most recognized fictional characters in the world. Jerry Siegel (left) was writing mystery stories as a high school student when he created Superman, and Joe Shuster (right) did the early drawings. It took the pair until 1938 to find a publisher, New Fun Comics (Detective Comics), which published the comic strip in *Action Comics*, No. 1, June 1938.

D.A. LEVY. Darryl Allen Levy (1942–1968), a native Clevelander, was a poet popular in the counterculture movement and underground press during the 1960s. Levy wrote about social injustice, repression, and freedom of expression, all familiar themes of the anti-establishment class. Levy published Cleveland's first underground newspaper, *The Buddhist Third Class Junkmail Oracle* and published *The Marijuana Quarterly*, which called for the legalization of the drug. In 1968, Levy committed suicide. (Photograph by Tom Prusha.)

THE CLEVELAND PRESS. Louis B. Seltzer was the longtime editor of *The Cleveland Press*, Cleveland's leading newspaper, and both he and the publication took many top honors in the field of print journalism. The last issue of the *Press* was published June 17, 1982. Here is the Cleveland Press Building, located on the northeast corner of East 9th Street and Lakeside Avenue. It was razed to make room for the 20-story North Point Office Complex.

THE CLEVELAND HEALTH MUSEUM. When the Cleveland Health Museum opened to the public on November 13, 1940, it had the honor of being America's first permanent health museum. The museum's mission was to educate the public about all matters concerning health through exhibits, demonstrations, and classes. The museum, located at 8911 Euclid Avenue, has undergone extensive remodeling since this 1966 photograph when it still resembled a mansion. (Photograph by Clayton Knipper.)

MEET THE VISIBLE WOMAN. One of the most popular exhibits at the Cleveland Health Museum, particularly for children, is the "Visible Woman." Here, in 1964, junior volunteer Steve Helper shows off the transparent woman to a group of children from the University Settlement House. Cleveland was the only city to receive a talking model that instructs visitors in the workings of her inner organs, all 24 of them, which light up as she speaks. (Photograph by Herman Seid.)

MEET HAPPY! One of the most popular attractions at the Cleveland Museum of Natural History can be found in Kirtland Hall. It is Happy the Haplocanthosaurus, and at 120 million years old, it is still able to draw the crowds. Happy is on display in this photograph in 1977 with other fossil, skeletal, and prehistoric discoveries on the main floor.

THE CLEVELAND MUSEUM OF NATURAL HISTORY. The first permanent home of the Natural History Museum is seen here in the former mansion of Cleveland philanthropist Leonard Hanna located on Euclid Avenue. In 1958, the mansion was razed to make room for a freeway overpass, and plans for a new museum to be built in University Circle were laid. In 1961, the new museum was unveiled to include galleries, an observatory, a research library, and a planetarium.

MAGNIFICENT SEVERANCE HALL. One of the jewels of University Circle, Cleveland's cultural district, Severance Hall is located on the corner of East Boulevard and Euclid Avenue. It was dedicated in 1931 and seats 1,844 patrons in the main concert hall. Designed by the Cleveland architectural firm Walker & Weeks, Severance also has a chamber music hall called Reinberger Hall, which seats 400 patrons.

THE CORNERSTONE OF CULTURE. On May 3, 1930, industrialist and philanthropist John L. Severance stood beside the cornerstone to Severance Hall, which was built from his generous donation of $4 million as the permanent home of the Cleveland Orchestra. Joining Severance was socialite Adella Prentiss Hughes, who organized the orchestra and is turned looking towards businessman and philanthropist Dudley S. Blossom (with hand in pocket).

84

GEORGE SZELL AND THE CLEVELAND ORCHESTRA. George Szell conducts the Cleveland Orchestra at Severance Hall during the 1969 season. Mr. Szell served as musical director and conductor of the Cleveland Orchestra from 1946 until his death in 1970. During Mr. Szell's tenure, the orchestra undertook an extensive series of successful American and foreign tours that enhanced its reputation and established it as one of the world's great symphonic orchestra's.

WCLV-FM. Since 1962, WCLV has been Cleveland's principal fine arts radio station. Its program, "WCLV Saturday Night," was Cleveland's longest running program on a single radio station. Since 1965, WCLV has broadcast performances of the Cleveland Orchestra. Here, in 1966, Robert Conrad, the Orchestra's radio voice, adjusts the controls in the Severance Hall recording booth. With him are Mrs. Edwin Hoffman and Mrs. David Murray Jr. (Photograph by Frank Reed.)

THE CLEVELAND WOMEN'S ORCHESTRA. Seventy women comprise the Cleveland Women's Orchestra, and a section of the group is seen here in March of 1951 during a rehearsal with longtime conductor and violinist with the Cleveland Orchestra, Hyman Schandler. The Women's Orchestra was created in 1935 in response to the small representation of women in professional symphonic orchestras. The Women's Orchestra travels to deliver performances in a variety of venues. (Photograph by Clayton Knipper.)

THE CLEVELAND INSTITUTE OF MUSIC. In May of 1970, students of the Cleveland Institute of Music (CIM) on French horns presented an outdoor performance called "Brass on the Grass." Located in University Circle on East Boulevard and Hazel Drive, the CIM, seen here, was completed in 1961 and was equipped with a concert hall, classrooms, studios, and a library. The CIM continues to offer the finest programs in music education for children, teens, and adults. (Photograph by Frank Reed.)

Six

MEDIA STARS AND LOCAL TALENT

THE ' KINGS. Cleveland's strong ethnic base made this local variety show featuring polka bands a staple of Sunday afternoon programming. What began in 1957 as *The Frankie Yankovic Show* on WEWS Channel 5 at 1 p.m. became the very popular *Polka Varieties Show* featuring Paul Wilcox (left) as host and band favorites Herman Spero, Al Herrick, and on accordion, Polka great Frank Yankovic.

THE DEBUT OF STATION WEWS. On December 17, 1947, actor James Steward (left) was the opening night star as WEWS Channel 5, a Scripps-Howard television station, opened in Cleveland. Jack R. Howard (center) was president of Scripps-Howard Radio, and James C. Hahrahan (right) was general manager of WEWS. The first WEWS program televised Stewart's appearance as master of ceremonies at the *Cleveland Press* Christmas show. (Acme Newspictures.)

BILL GORDON GETS PINNED. Formerly a radio personality from WHR, Bill Gordon joined WEWS Channel 5's Dorothy Fuldheim on her *The One O'Clock Club* show, which aired from 1957 to 1964. Here, Bill and Dorothy are joined by Boy Scout executive John Shanks (in glasses) and a troop of scouts on a special Saturday morning edition of the show on March 3, 1962, promoting Greater Cleveland's Boy Scout Drive. *The One O'Clock Club* normally aired Monday through Friday.

CLEVELAND'S OWN DOROTHY FULDHEIM. There is perhaps no television personality more closely associated with Cleveland broadcasting than Dorothy Fuldheim (June 26, 1893–November 3, 1989). Her association with WEWS Channel 5, which she joined just months before its debut in 1947, placed her at the forefront of women broadcasters when she became the first woman in America to have her own news show. Her strong personality and sharp interviewing skills made *The One O'Clock Club* a hit, as she interviewed countless celebrities. In this photograph, entertainer Bob Hope chats with Dorothy during the first of five scheduled appearances about his new book, which was being serialized in *The Cleveland Press*. Bob Hope grew up in Cleveland, and in recognition of his star status and his family's contribution in helping construct the Lorain-Carnegie Bridge, it was re-named the Hope Memorial Bridge. In addition to reviewing books on her show, Dorothy traveled the world as a reporter for WEWS and appeared daily as a commentator for the local evening news. Dorothy's last interview occurred in 1984 with President Ronald Reagan.

HAPPY BIRTHDAY GENE CARROLL! In April of 1948, Gene Carroll (April 13, 1897–March 5, 1972) debuted as host of what would become one of the longest running variety shows in the country, *The Gene Carroll Show*, which aired on WEWS Channel 5 on Sunday, from noon to 1p.m. Here, Gene poses with Andrea Carroll (no relation) as the show celebrates its 16th season. Andrea's success on the show led to a recording contract and several hit songs.

SCHOLASTIC TELEVISION. On February 5, 1962 at 8:45 a.m., Miss Deloras Fratus, appearing on closed-circuit television, lectured on art appreciation to fourth graders at Scranton School on Cleveland's west side. It was the first lesson taught to Cleveland school children via Classroom T.V., an innovative teaching program pioneered by WEWS Channel 5.

IT'S ACADEMIC! Local WEWS Channel 5 personality Don Webster served as the host of *It's Academic*, the high school quiz show consisting of three-student teams in a three-school competition. Here, Webster welcomes students from South High School in Cleveland. The show debuted in 1964 with host Don Cameron. Webster took over as host in 1971. The show, renamed *Academic Challenge*, remains on Saturday night with current host Adam Shapiro.

THE MORNING EXCHANGE VISITS SEA WORLD. *The Morning Exchange* on WEWS Channel 5, with hosts (left to right) Fred Griffiths, Liz Richards, and Joel Rose, ruled local morning programming by offering a variety of informational, news, and talk-format entertainment. *The Morning Exchange* is often considered the forerunner of the nationally televised *Good Morning America* program. In this photograph, the morning trio pose with Shamu, the killer whale, at Sea World aquatic park in Aurora, Ohio.

MISS BARBARA AND FRIENDS. Barbara Plummer celebrated her seventh year as teacher / host of *Romper Room* with friends (left to right) Flint Keller, Kim Humphrey and Marge Smith, who together presented Miss Barbara with a floral arrangement. *Romper Room* was a popular half-hour kids' show on WEWS Channel 5, weekday mornings. She always ended her show by holding a "magic mirror" and asking "Have all my friends had fun at play?"

CAPTAIN PENNY'S FUN HOUSE. Ron "Captain Penny" Penfound (standing) and Earl "Wilbur Wiffenpoof" Keyes (at piano) pose for the premier of the new kids show *Captain Penny's Fun House* on WEWS Channel 5. The show aired weekdays at 6 p.m. and featured skits and the Little Rascals' movies. Ron Penfound came to Cleveland from Colorado where he worked as a radio announcer. Joining the Captain and Wilbur is "Bobo," one of their many zany friends who helped make the show a favorite for kids.

"TELL THEM BARNABY SAYS HELLO!" Children's programming was not limited to one Cleveland station. Perhaps one of the most enduring kids' personalities was "Barnaby" the leprechaun, portrayed by actor Linn Sheldon, who lived in the "Enchanted Forest" on WKYC Channel 3. *Barnaby* aired seven days a week and became the most popular kids show in town. In this 1959 photograph, Barnaby welcomes Boy Scouts (left to right) Jeremy Hudson, Johnny Eagen, and Frank Cole as his guests.

FRANZ THE TOYMAKER AND FRIENDS. A latecomer to children's programming was Ray Stawiarski, who debuted in the early 1960s on WJW Channel 8 as "Franz" in *Franz the Toymaker*. In this 1967 photograph, Franz is dressed in German costume, and in a convincing German accent, he addresses the crowd gathered for a radio-sponsored event. The half-hour show ran weekday mornings.

WJW-TV Adds Color to Television. On March 1, 1964, Cleveland Mayor Ralph S. Locher (left) assisted WJW-TV General Manager Robert S. Buchanan (right) in pushing the "color button" to officially start Cleveland's first locally originated program in color. The ceremonies took place at 4 p.m. in the station's studios, as WJW Channel 8 planned to present over 90 hours of local programming in color for Cleveland viewers.

Ghoulardi! Before he became "the voice" of ABC-TV, Ernie Anderson (center) was known locally as "Ghoulardi," the irreverent and slightly crazed Friday night host of horror movies that aired on WJW Channel 8. Ghoulardi developed a cult-like following as he injected his own brand of humor (and himself) into fright flicks to the amusement of Cleveland viewers. In this 1964 Thanksgiving Parade, Anderson is flanked by parade marshal John Bellas (left) and Mayor James Day (right) of Parma, or as Ghoulardi would say, "Amrap."

THE GHOULARDI ALL STARS. In this 1966 photograph, Ernie "Ghoulardi" Anderson (front row, third from left) lends his name to the WJW-TV 8 baseball team playing for charity. Anderson was arguably the most popular Channel 8 personality thanks to his offbeat character, "Ghoulardi." Some of the more popular personalities in the WJW line-up are weather forecaster Dick Goddard (front row, second from left) and Ray "Franz the Toymaker" Stawiarski (back row, fourth from left).

BIG CHUCK AND LITTLE JOHN. When Ernie Anderson left for Hollywood in 1966, taking the inimitable "Ghoulardi" character with him, the void for Friday night horror host was filled by the team of Big Chuck Schodowski (right) and Little John Rinaldi (left). They were known simply as "Big Chuck and Little John." They came together in 1979 and have been entertaining audiences for years with their zany skits and parodies.

RADIO STATION WGAR. In this December 1939 photograph, radio station reporter Jack Parr (left) interviews actor George Raft, who was visiting Cleveland. WGAR was one of a handful of stations airing in Cleveland; it debuted in 1930 from the Hotel Statler. Jack Parr was one of many celebrities who got their first break in Cleveland before achieving national prominence. (Photograph by Walter Kneal.)

ENTERTAINING THE TROOPS. In 1952, as soldiers waited for trains at Cleveland's USO Lounge located in the Terminal Tower, WJW 850 radio disc jockeys Jack Clifton (left) and Soupy Hines (right), better known as "Soupy Sales," entertain them with direct broadcasts from the lounge. Here, Jack and Soupy play some favorites for two Air Force servicemen on their way home for Christmas leave. Joining the group are USO Special Events Chairwomen Mrs. Edward Neff (left) and Mrs. George Fisher (right).

CLEVELAND'S NUMBER ONE DISC JOCKEY. Bill Randle arrived in Cleveland in 1949 as a disc jockey for radio station WERE 1300 AM. He quickly became a national leader in promoting recorded jazz and early rock n' roll and was the first to introduce the young Elvis Presley above the Mason-Dixon Line. The holder of six college degrees, Dr. William McKinley Randle Jr., or Bill Randle, also managed successful careers as an educator, being a professor of history at Fenn College, and as a lawyer, in between his stints as a popular radio deejay.

THE MOON DOG CORONATION BALL. A crowd of over 25,000 attended what rock n' roll historians consider the first rock n' roll concert, the Moon Dog Coronation Ball at the Cleveland Arena held March 22, 1952. Organized by Alan "Moon Dog" Freed, the WJW-AM radio disc jockey, who with Leo Mintz, coined the term "rock n' roll," the concert gave instant national celebrity to obscure rhythm n' blues artists and put rock n' roll music on the map. (Photograph by Peter Hastings.)

CLEVELAND MEETS THE BEATLES! On September 15, 1964, The Beatles, John Lennon (in glasses), George Harrison, Paul McCartney, and Ringo Starr, landed at Cleveland-Hopkins International Airport from Pittsburgh shortly after midnight. They came to play at Public Hall in downtown Cleveland, with radio station WHK sponsoring the show. To the dismay of hundreds of fans at the airport, The Beatles managed to slip away to the Sheraton-Cleveland Hotel on Public Square. (Photograph by Tony Tomsic.)

THE BEATLES PLAY PUBLIC HALL. When the Beatles performed at 8 p.m. before more than 11,000 screaming fans (mostly girls), hysteria moved fans to rush the stage as 500 Cleveland police officers worked to keep them back. Across the bottom of the stage is one long row of policemen, an overbearing presence that The Beatles complained about. For the first time in Beatle concert history, the show had to be stopped for 10 minutes to quiet the surge of fans. (Photograph by Tony Tomsic.)

CLEVELANDERS WELCOME THE GRASSHOPPERS. Don Webster (far right) hosted the *Big Five Show* on WEWS Channel 5, which aired on Saturday afternoon at 5 p.m. The show featured popular recording artists of the 1960s. Here, Paul Anka (seated at piano) plays with The Grasshoppers, a Cleveland group with a Beatle sound.

WIXY 1260 RADIO. If one radio station rocked during the 1960s, it was WIXY 1260. Clevelanders fondly remember the "Top-100 Countdown of New Year's Eve" with the list of the top rock n' roll tunes published in the *Showtime Magazine* of *The Cleveland Press*. In July of 1972, WIXY celebrated staff appreciation day with (left to right) disc jockey Jeff McKee, singer-songwriter Buffy St. Marie, WIXY Program Director Chuck Dunaway, and General Manager Gene Taylor (behind Dunaway).

PINK FLOYD ROCKS MUNICIPAL STADIUM. The Beatles led the way of the British invasion, which brought many of their countrymen like Pink Floyd to America, and eventually to Cleveland. Due in part to the influence and rock format of radio station WMMS, Cleveland was seen as a major arena for rock performers. Here, tens of thousands of die-hard fans jam the stadium in the summer of 1977 to hear Pink Floyd. (Photograph by Frank Reed.)

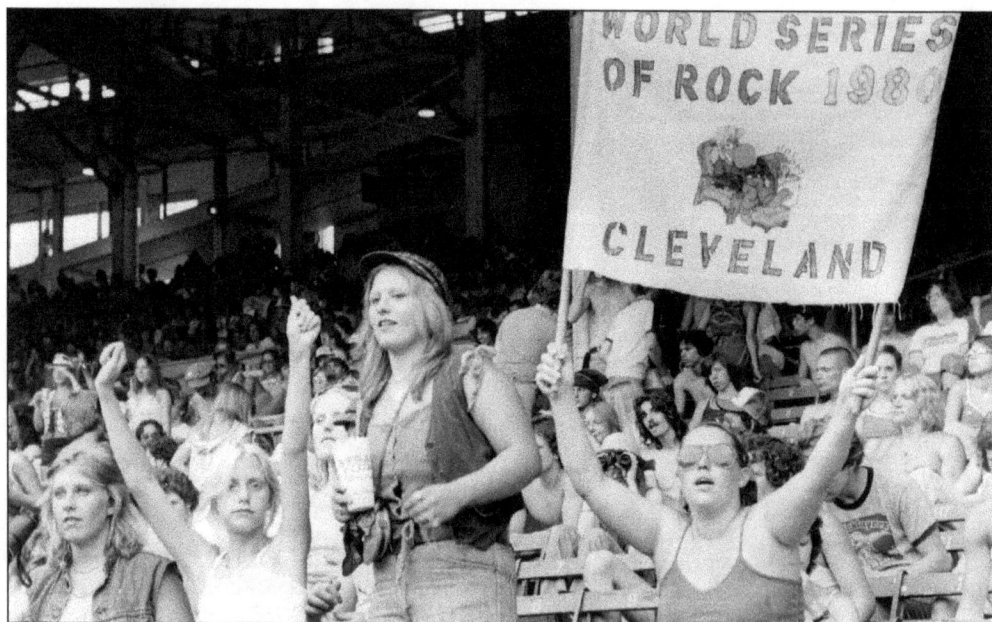

CLEVELAND ROCKS! In mid-July of 1980, Cleveland played host to an event called the World Series of Rock held at Cleveland Municipal Stadium. Radio station WMMS sponsored the event, which featured the finest acts in rock. WMMS, which broadcasts at 100.7 FM, once had a reputation as the premier rock station in the country. The trademark WMMS "Buzzard" is centered on the banner, held by an enthusiastic fan. (Photograph by Doug Mastroianni.)

Seven

THE SPORTS SCENE

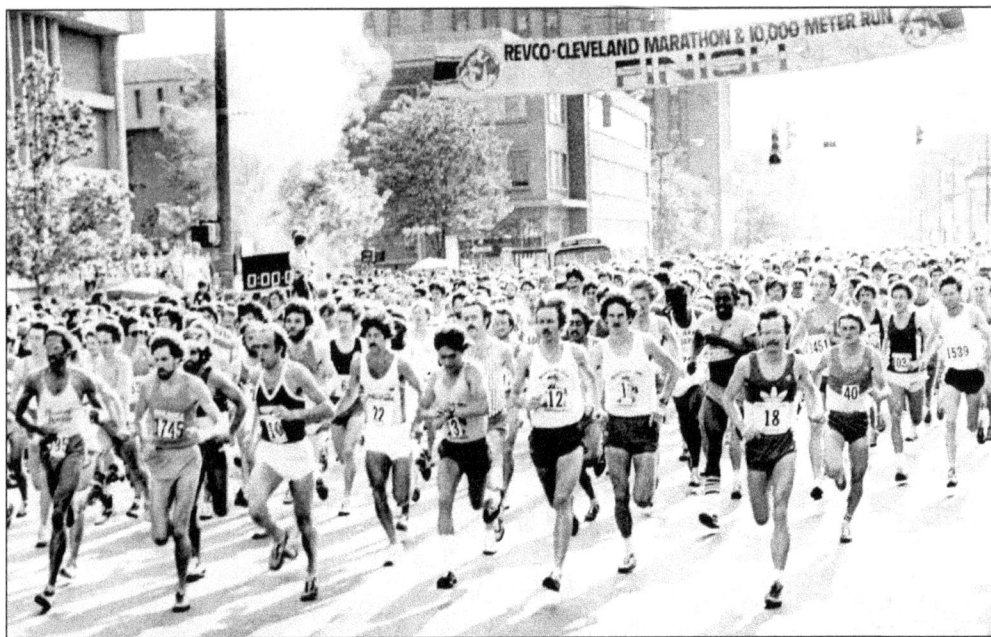

THE REVCO-CLEVELAND MARATHON. In May of 1979, 1,644 persons entered to compete in the annual Revco-Cleveland Marathon (26 miles) and 10,000 meter run. It was a major race, which attracted the finest runners nationally and worldwide. Cleveland State University, pictured here, was the starting and ending point as runners proceeded down Euclid Avenue, past Public Square, and out to the suburbs until they reached the turnaround point in Bay Village. Revco Discount Drug Stores sponsored the race. (Photograph by Tony Tomsic.)

THE BENDIX AIR RACE. Beginning in 1929, air races were organized as a means of promoting the airplane as the newest form of public transportation. Races were often sponsored by private companies like the Bendix Corporation, whose cross-country race attracted some of the finest talent in aviation. In this 1935 photograph, (left to right) , co-pilot Paul Mants, pilot Amelia Earhart, and airplane engine designer Al Monasco pose at the Cleveland leg of the race.

THE NATIONAL AIR RACES. Cleveland became the host city for the National Air Races, which spanned a period of 20 years, from 1929 to 1949. Cleveland's newly constructed Municipal Airport (later re-named Cleveland-Hopkins International Airport) was the location of the National Air Races, which, as seen here in 1932, drew record crowds eager to watch the daring feats of airplane and pilot.

PUBLIC SQUARE HOSPITALITY WEEK. Clevelanders have always enjoyed air shows and races and any opportunity to examine the latest in air travel. In this photograph taken around 1938, a crowd takes a look at a GL 1 plane, which appears on Public Square in front of Cleveland College courtesy of the Great Lakes Aircraft Corporation. The plane was part of a week-long celebration that welcomed the shrine and recognized Cleveland as a city of aviation.

BURKE LAKEFRONT AIRPORT. Named in honor of former Cleveland Mayor Thomas Burke, Burke Lakefront Airport is the city's second municipally owned airport, and its location on the lakefront serves to relieve the major Cleveland Hopkins International Airport of congestion by accommodating smaller planes. Burke also played host to a number of air shows, as seen here in 1979, where a crowd has gathered to inspect a navy Grumman tracker, which was used to locate submarines. (Photograph by Frank Reed.)

CLEVELAND'S SIX-DAY BIKE RACE. Cleveland was a popular location for all kinds of races and sporting events. Here, in 1933, Mildred "Babe" Didrickson, female Olympic champion (standing, left) prepares to officially start the International Six-Day Bike Race at Cleveland's Public Auditorium on January 20th. Racing stars like Reggie McNamara, a 26-year veteran of the racing ovals, and William "Torchy" Peden of Canada were among those in the starting lineup. (Acme Newspictures.)

STRAIGHT SHOOTERS. In the summer of 1953, 40 children competed in The Press-Greater Cleveland Marbles Tournament finals held at Municipal Stadium. Kneeling and shooting first were (left to right) Gerald Mehalko, 13, Warsaw Playground; Robert Lehman, 9, Gracemount Playground; Richard Kovach, 12, Hodge Playground; and George Ward, 11, Stafford Playground. The champion boy and girl would compete in the National Marbles Tournament at Asbury Park, New Jersey.

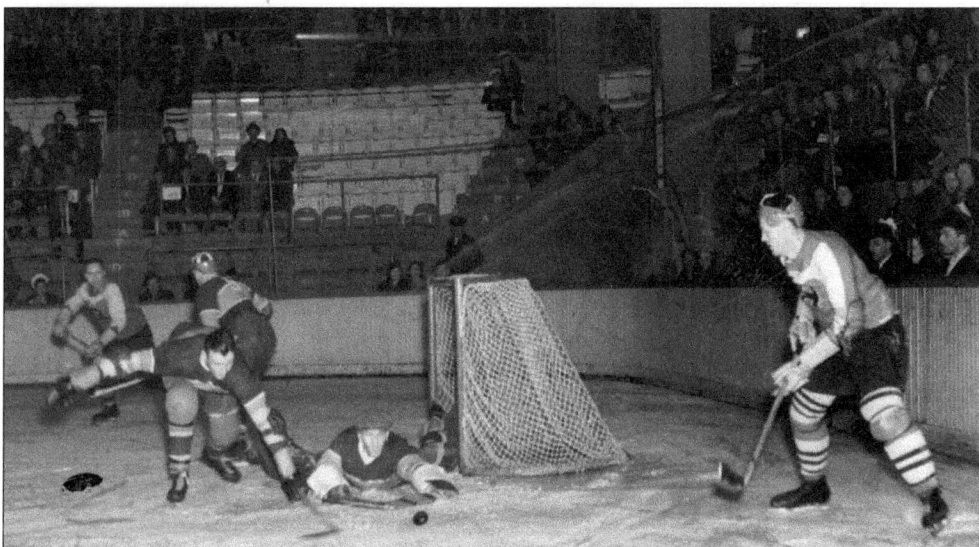

THE CLEVELAND BARONS. The Cleveland Arena was built as the home of the Cleveland Barons ice hockey team. Albert C. Sutphin, club owner, raised the $1.5 million required to build the arena. This 1938 photograph captures the Barons playing against the New Haven Eagles during their first season in the new arena. They won 2-0. It was one of a long string of wins for this once very popular and successful hockey franchise. (Photograph by Herman Seid.)

THE CLEVELAND ARENA. In this 1942 photograph, the Cleveland Arena is seen at its location at 3717 Euclid Avenue. The arena opened in 1937 with a seating capacity of 10,000 to host not only sporting events but also various forms of entertainment, which attracted local, national, and international celebrities. At its height, the arena hosted nearly 400 events annually. In 1977, the arena was razed. (Photograph by James Meli.)

Jesse Owens Conquers Berlin! Olympic great Jesse Owens (September 9, 1913–March 30, 1980), fresh from his victory in the 100-meter dash, signs autographs for admiring German spectators during the 1936 Olympics Games in Berlin. The four-time gold medalist, dubbed the fastest human, became a fan favorite as he won medals in the 100- and 200-meter races, the long jump, and the 400-meter relay. Raised in Cleveland, Owens distinguished himself in track and field while at Ohio State University. (Acme Newspictures.)

Harrison Dillard, World's Fastest Human. In 1948, native Clevelander William Harrison Dillard (July 8, 1923–) stands atop of the winner's rostrum at Empire Stadium in London after he tied the Olympic record of 10.3 seconds in the 100-meter dash. A student of Baldwin-Wallace College in Berea, Ohio, Dillard was joined by fellow teammate Barney Ewell of Lancaster, Pennsylvania, who finished in second place, and Lloyd LaBeach of Panama, who finished third. Dillard distinguished himself as the only athlete to win an Olympic gold in a sprint and a hurdle event. Like Owens, Dillard was the fastest human in his time. (Acme Newspictures.)

CLEVELAND INDIANS V. NEW YORK YANKEES. The rivalry between the Indians and the Yankees extends way back to when *The Cleveland Press* kept a baseball scoreboard on Public Square to keep anxious fans who were willing to brave bad weather current on the performance of their beloved team. (Photograph by Fred Bottomer.)

CLEVELAND INDIANS WIN THE WORLD SERIES! In 1948, Cleveland Indians fans watched the baseball club ride past Terminal Tower on Public Square in a parade held to honor their World Series victory against the Boston Braves, winning four games to two. Waving to enthusiastic fans in the lead car were club owner Bill Veeck (right) and shortstop / manager Lou Boudreau (left). This was the last time the Cleveland Indians would win the World Series.

107

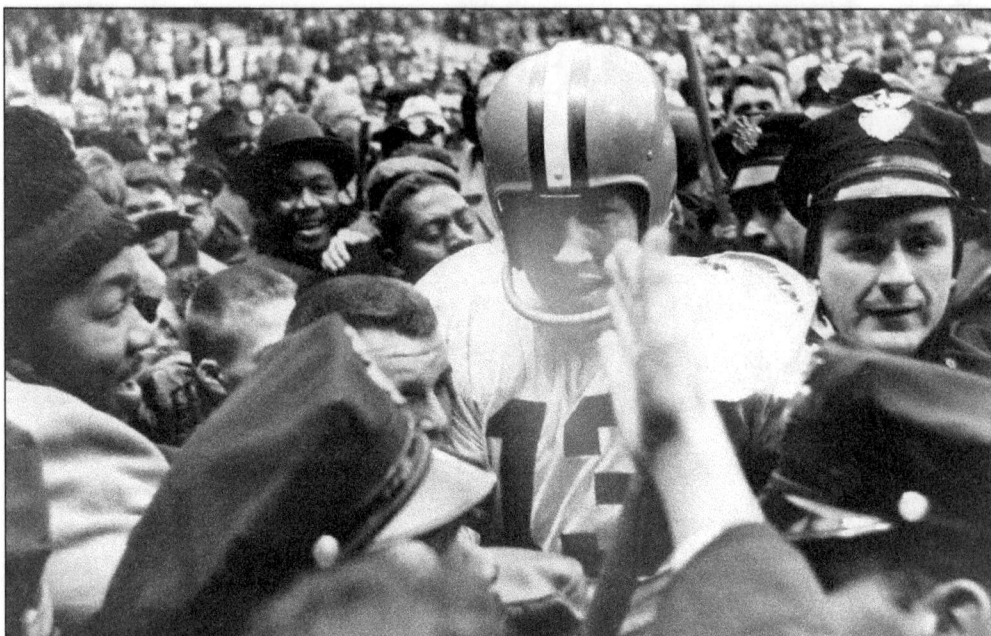

CLEVELAND BROWNS AS NFL CHAMPS. On December 27, 1964, the Cleveland Browns played the Baltimore Colts for the National Football League Championship and won with a score of 27-0. Led by head coach Blanton Collier, Number 13 quarterback Frank Ryan successfully threw three touchdown passes to receiver Gary Collins to shut the Colts down. This was the last time the Cleveland Browns reigned as football champions. (Photograph by Bernie Noble.)

CLEVELAND'S GOOD FORTUNE. The success of the Cleveland Browns at the National Football League Championships inspired famed director Billy Wilder (far lower right in black hat, opposite the camera) to use Cleveland and the team as the basis for his comedy film, *The Fortune Cookie*, released in 1966. St. Vincent Charity Hospital, pictured here, was used as the fictional St. Mark's Hospital. (Photograph by Jerry Horton.)

THE CHAMPIONSHIP RAMS. In December of 1945, the Cleveland Rams football club, led by (left to right) Jim Gillette, quarterback Bob Waterfield, Jim Benton, and head coach Adam Walsh, delivered the team's best season ever as they defeated the Washington Redskins to win the NFL Championship. The Rams were Cleveland's first NFL franchise team before the Cleveland Browns. Despite a championship season, the Rams left in 1946 for Los Angeles.

MONDAY NIGHT FOOTBALL. Cleveland Municipal Stadium was the site of the first Monday Night Football game televised on September 21, 1970, when the Cleveland Browns beat the New York Jets 31-21. In this photograph, Cleveland linebacker Jim Houston intercepts a pass by quarterback Joe Namath in the second quarter to give the Browns the lead. (Photograph by Paul Tepley.)

THE CLEVELAND PIPERS. The Cleveland Pipers, a Cleveland basketball club, won the national championship as members of the American Athletic Union during the 1960–1961 season. Pictured here are (left to right, in front) Coach John McLendon, Joe Wise, Ron Hamilton, Jim McCoy, and Tony Windis; and (left to right, in back) Dick Berghoff, Doyle Edmiston, Corny Freeman, Gene Tormohlen, Ralph Crosthwaite, Chuck Curtis, and Delton Heard.

STEINBRENNER PAYS FOR THE PIPERS. In 1961, George Steinbrenner, current owner of the New York Yankees, was a fixture in Cleveland sports when he purchased the Cleveland Pipers basketball club to join the newly formed American Basketball League, of which Cleveland belonged to the Eastern Division. Pictured here are (left to right) George Steinbrenner, Larry Siegfried and father George Siegfried, and Piper Coach John McLendon.

Cleveland Honors Robert Manry. Robert N. Manry (June 3, 1918–February 21, 1971), a copy editor for *The Plain Dealer* newspaper, made nautical history in 1965 when he crossed the Atlantic Ocean in his 13.5-foot ship christened *Tinkerbelle*. The trip from Falmouth, Massachusetts, to Falmouth, England, took two and a half months. In September of 1965, Mayor Ralph Locher (right) honored Manry (left) before an admiring crowd on Public Square. (Photograph by Paul Tepley.)

Tinkerbelle **Sails into Falmouth.** On August 17, 1965, Robert Manry realized his dream when he arrived in England's Falmouth Harbor and succeeded in his quest to cross the Atlantic nonstop, in 78 days, in what many viewed as the smallest sailboat ever to complete the 3,200-mile trip. Manry was greeted on shore by his wife and children. He wrote of his Atlantic crossing in a book titled *Tinkerbelle*. The sailboat is now part of the permanent collection of the Western Reserve Historical Society in Cleveland. (United Press International photograph.)

THE BROWNS FINAL GAME. On December 17, 1995, the Cleveland Browns played their final football game at Cleveland's Municipal Stadium. They played against the Cincinnati Bengals and won 26–10. Shortly thereafter, team owner Art Modell made the bold and controversial move of relocating the team to Baltimore, where the Browns became the Baltimore Ravens. The Browns name and colors remained in Cleveland. (Photograph by David Kachinko.)

MUNICIPAL STADIUM RAZED. In this aerial photograph taken in 1997, the remains of Cleveland Municipal Stadium appear like a giant crater as it awaits construction of the new stadium, which will be home to the new Cleveland Browns, an expansion team, originally owned by the late millionaire businessman Al Lerner. His son Randy assumed ownership upon his father's death. (Photograph by David Kachinko.)

112

Eight

MOVING TOWARDS THE 21ST CENTURY

THE GATEWAY SPORTS ENTERTAINMENT COMPLEX. In 1994, Cleveland welcomed its newest sports and entertainment complex, Gateway, located on the corner of Huron Road and Ontario Avenue, which includes Jacobs Field, home of the Cleveland Indians, and Gund Arena, home of the Cleveland Cavaliers basketball team. The demolition of Municipal Stadium gave baseball a separate home from the Browns, and Gund Arena replaced the Cleveland Arena and the Richfield Coliseum as the Cavaliers' home.

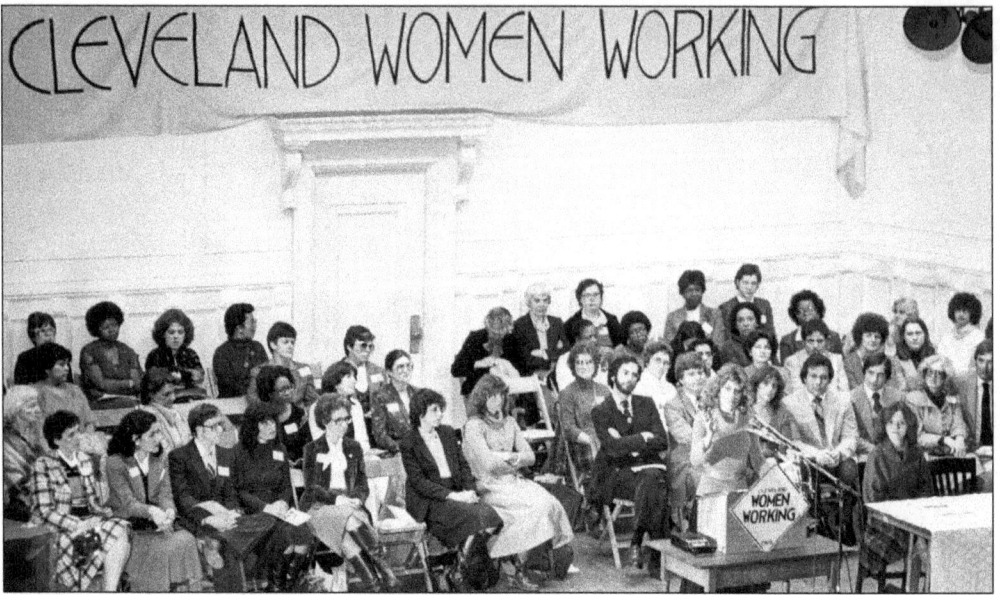

CLEVELAND WOMEN WORKING. Cleveland had always been a popular venue for various advocacy and political groups to meet and promote their agenda. In December of 1979, an enthusiastic crowd listened to actress-turned-activist Jane Fonda addressing the Cleveland Women Working organization in the auditorium of the Engineers Building downtown. CWW was created in 1975 with the purpose of securing equal rights and equal pay for working women. (Photograph by Tim Culek.)

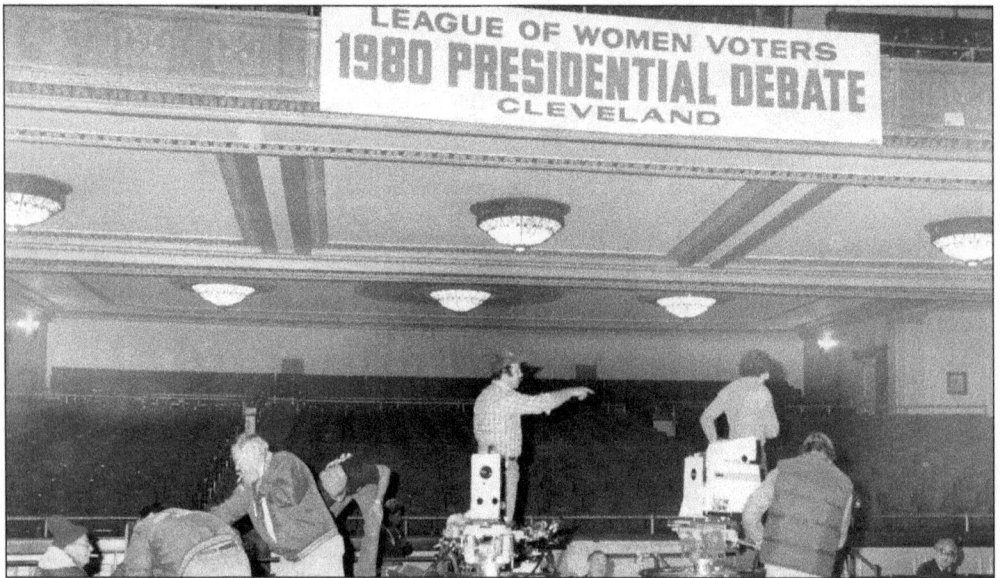

CLEVELAND'S LEAGUE OF WOMEN VOTERS. In October of 1980, the League of Women Voters of Cleveland served as host to the 1980 Presidential Debate between incumbent Jimmy Carter and Republican challenger Ronald Reagan held at the Music Hall in downtown Cleveland. The nonpartisan League of Women Voters was created in 1920 during the women's suffragette movement to secure the vote for all women. The League is active today and maintains offices on Euclid Avenue. (Photograph by Bernie Noble.)

114

THE 1980 PRESIDENTIAL DEBATE. Cleveland was placed favorably in the national spotlight in 1980 when it was selected as the host city for the televised presidential debate. In this scene, a jubilant President Carter waves to a crowd of supporters. He is joined at the podium by Ohio Democratic Senator and former Mercury astronaut John Glenn. The NASA Glenn Research Center in Cleveland was named in his honor. At the far right is first lady Rosalind Carter. (Photograph by Bernie Noble.)

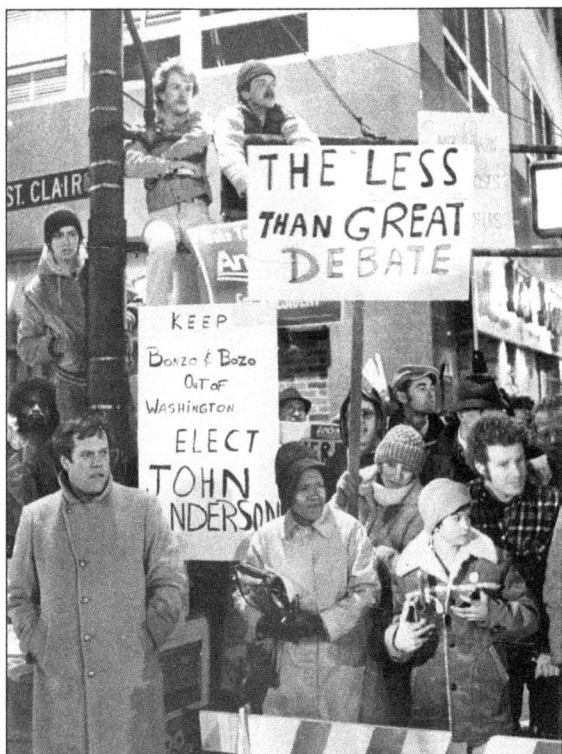

THE LESS THAN GREAT DEBATE. Clevelanders have never been shy about voicing their support or expressing dissent toward political candidates. The televised debates turned the spotlight on everyday Clevelanders who, as shown by the crowd seen here on St. Clair Avenue downtown, would like to elect John Anderson as the next president. The message, "Keep Bonzo & Bozo out of Washington" refers to Republican candidate Reagan and his running mate George Bush Sr. (Photograph by Tony Tomsic.)

UNIVERSITY HOSPITALS OF CLEVELAND. This aerial view of University Hospitals of Cleveland was taken in 1996. Cleveland has several outstanding world-class hospitals, and University Hospitals is one of them. It is a not-for-profit teaching and research facility linked to the School of Medicine at Case Western Reserve University, now known simply as Case. UH is located near Case on Euclid Avenue in the area of University Circle. (Photograph by David Kachinko.)

ST. VINCENT CHARITY HOSPITAL. St. Vincent opened in August of 1965 on East 22nd Street as Cleveland's newest urban hospital. It is a Catholic medical and teaching hospital owned by the Sisters of Charity of St. Augustine Health System and University Hospitals Health System. The ultramodern seven-story gently curved structure seen here was built at a cost of $5 million. St. Vincent is a pioneer in the field of bloodless surgery and medicine and in bariatric surgery. (Photograph by Herman Seid.)

THE CLEVELAND CLINIC. Seen here in 1980, the Cleveland Clinic has a national and an international reputation as one of the finest medical and research hospitals, being consistently ranked number one in the field of cardiac care. The Cleveland Clinic stretches for several city blocks, from East 88th to East 105th Streets and from Chester to Cedar Avenues. This not-for-profit facility is one of Cleveland's largest employers with over 8,000 workers in professional and support positions. (Photograph by Larry Nighswander.)

METROHEALTH MEDICAL CENTER. The MetroHealth Medical Center is a world-class medical and teaching facility located on the west side of Cleveland. As seen in this 1996 aerial, it is a sprawling 731-bed complex nestled between West 25th Street and Scranton Road, also known as MetroHealth Drive. Since 1914, it has been affiliated with the Case Western Reserve University School of Medicine. MetroHealth is noted for its outstanding burn unit and its many community outreach programs. (Photograph by David Kachinko.)

CUYAHOGA COMMUNITY COLLEGE. Cuyahoga Community College, or "Tri-C," was created to meet the need for low cost, convenient, academic and skill-oriented training among minorities, women, displaced workers, and older students. Chartered in 1962, its first classes were held in the fall of 1963 at the Brownell School Building at East 14th Street and Brownell Court. The Metropolitan Campus downtown, seen here, opened in 1966.

CASE WESTERN RESERVE UNIVERSITY. In 1964, Case Institute of Technology and Western Reserve University agreed to merge and initiated the process that led to the creation of Case Western Reserve University in 1967. This 1969 aerial view shows the Case campus along East Boulevard at the top center and part of the WRU campus and University Hospitals to the left in University Circle.

118

CLEVELAND STATE UNIVERSITY. Cleveland State University, or CSU, is a comprehensive, urban university located on 83 acres in downtown Cleveland. It was established in 1964 as a state-assisted university to provide public higher education for residents of Cleveland and Northeast Ohio. In 1965, the university acquired the buildings, faculty, and programs of Fenn College, a private institution of 2,500 students. By September of 1965, CSU held its first classes. Today, CSU's seven colleges offer undergraduate degrees in 70 major fields, 27 master's degree programs, two post-master's degrees, six doctoral, and two law degrees. In 1991, the CSU Convocation Center was opened to provide a recreation center to host sporting events, as well as concerts and other attractions of public interest. The Convocation Center appears near the bottom left of this aerial view taken in 1996, which looks north from East 18th Street to the Interstate 90 Inner Beltway. Towards the middle left of the view rises the 19-story Rhodes Tower, so-named for former Ohio Governor James Rhodes. Faculty and graduate offices, the library and archives, and classrooms occupy Rhodes Tower. (Photograph by David Kachinko.)

THE JUSTICE CENTER AND PORTAL. The Cuyahoga County Justice Center is a 26-story tower atop an eight-story base at the southeast corner of Ontario and Lakeside Avenues. Completed in 1977, it houses the Cleveland Police Headquarters, common pleas court, municipal court, county prosecutor, probation office, and correction center. The sculpture, *Portal*, by Isamu Noguchi is located near the main entrance. Intended to suggest a gateway, the sculpture has never been warmly received by the public. (Photograph by Van Dillard.)

THE LAUSCHE STATE OFFICE BUILDING. Gracing the entrance to the Lausche Building, named in honor of former Cleveland Mayor, Governor of Ohio, and U.S. Senator Frank J. Lausche, is a monument titled *Last*. The angled steel arch, painted orange, was created by sculptor Tony Smith, seen here in 1980 with his wife, Jane. (Photograph by Bernie Noble.)

IMPLOSION ON PUBLIC SQUARE. On October 3, 1982, two historic Cleveland landmarks, the Cuyahoga Building and the Williamson Building (seen on the cover of this book), were imploded in order to make room for the construction of the Sohio (later known as British Petroleum, or BP) Building. As seen here, the buildings begin to collapse in a cloud of thick black smoke, which gradually will engulf the area immediately around Public Square. The implosion drew many visitors downtown to witness the end of an era.

GOODBYE CUYAHOGA AND WILLIAMSON. The crowd widens around the Soldiers and Sailors Monument (seen right of center) as the dust begins to settle where the Cuyahoga and Williamson Buildings once stood. Groundbreaking ceremonies were not far off for the construction of the Sohio Building. The year of 1982 was also memorable for Cleveland because for the second time in its history, Cleveland was named an All-American City.

EAST BANK OF THE FLATS. Banking the sides of the Cuyahoga River is the area known as the Flats, which offers a variety of entertainment, particularly nightlife and summer fun. Here, in July of 1996, visitors enjoy dining at Landry's Seafood House, some docking their own boats by the diner. Spanning across the back is the Main Avenue Bridge, and the skyscrapers are (left to right) the Justice Center, Society Center Building, the BP Building, and the Terminal Tower. (Photograph by David Kachinko.)

WEST BANK OF THE FLATS. This July 1996 view of the Flats is taken from the west bank and highlights some of the seasonal fun enjoyed by the crowd. Pleasure boating on the Cuyahoga River attracted many who wished to show-off their craft. On the right, just below the Main Avenue Bridge, also called the Harold H. Burton Bridge, is the popular Shooters restaurant, one of the first to open on the boardwalk. (Photograph by David Kachinko.)

122

DINING ON THE EAST 9TH STREET PIER. One very popular dining spot that anchored the 9th Street Pier for more than 30 years was Captain Frank's Lobster House. It was the place to go not only for seafood creations but also for prime Angus steaks and specialty Italian cuisine. Captain Frank's is no longer a fixture on the pier but can be found in Cleveland's historic Warehouse District downtown. (Photograph by Bill Nehez.)

DOCKING AND DINING IN THE FLATS. This 1996 scene presents the east bank of the Flats south of the Main Avenue Bridge. The Watermark Restaurant was a popular attraction for diners, and docking one's craft on the Cuyahoga River as seen here was an all too common occurrence in summer. In the background, the Terminal Tower (right) and the BP Building (left) are partially visible. (Photograph by David Kachinko.)

THE FLATS AND WAREHOUSE DISTRICT. This breathtaking 1996 aerial view of Cleveland highlights the Flats and the Warehouse District. On the left is the Main Avenue Bridge, which leads the eye back to such lakefront attractions as the new Cleveland Browns Stadium (upper left corner), the Great Lakes Science Center, and the Rock and Roll Hall of Fame. At right is the Veterans Memorial Bridge. In the background is a cluster of Cleveland's tallest buildings. (Photograph by David Kachinko.)

ON THE RTA WATERFRONT LINE. The RTA Waterfront Line is a light rail system that travels 2.2 miles west of the Cuyahoga River and north along the shore of Lake Erie. It was built in 1996 to celebrate the bicentennial. The Waterfront Line was designed for tourists visiting lakefront attractions. Seen here are passengers boarding a train on East 9th Street at the North Coast Station, built for the tourist line. (Photograph by David Kachinko.)

124

CLEVELAND SKYLINE FROM OVER THE FLATS. This aerial view of the city was taken during the summer of the bicentennial. The tallest building in Cleveland is the Society Center Building, which stands 948.7 feet tall. It is followed by the BP Building, which stands between the Society Center Building and the Terminal Tower. (Photograph by David Kachinko.)

EAST 14TH STREET AND PROSPECT AVENUE. This aerial view was taken in September 1996 and highlights another area of downtown Cleveland. Seen in the right foreground is the Erie Street Cemetery. In between the trees, headstones appear as tiny white dots. Towards the center is the historic Playhouse Square District featuring the Ohio and State Theaters. (Photograph by David Kachinko.)

EASTBOUND ARRIVAL AT COLLINWOOD. Collinwood is one of Cleveland's better-known neighborhoods. It is located approximately seven miles northeast of Public Square. Since Collinwood was positioned near Lake Erie, it became a major switchyard for railroads like the New York Central. The view here looks west from the East 152nd Street Bridge as Conrail moves past a surviving coal tower. (Photograph by David Kachinko.)

CLEVELAND HOPKINS INTERNATIONAL AIRPORT. This is a 1996 aerial view of Cleveland's major airport, located on the city's west side approximately eight miles southwest of Public Square. Built in 1927 as Cleveland Municipal Airport, it was renamed in 1951 to honor William R. Hopkins, Cleveland's first city manager and the airport's founder. Cleveland Hopkins International Airport remains a major carrier of passenger and freight today and is one of the busiest airports in the Midwest. (Photograph by David Kachinko.)

BRIDGES MAKE THE CITY. Cleveland has always been defined by its waterways, be it the Cuyahoga River, seen here winding through the Flats, or the great Lake Erie. Spanning across the center page with steel-blue trusses is the Main Avenue Bridge. On the lower right is the Conrail Bridge with a "jackknife" bridge raised behind. Curving around the left is the Waterfront Line. In the background is the Veterans Memorial Bridge, Cleveland's first high-level bridge. (Photograph by David Kachinko.)

SUNSET IN CLEVELAND. Many Clevelanders enjoy the fact that the city is located along the shores of Lake Erie and is not landlocked. Here, two fishermen walk along a break wall jutting out into the lake. The sun is setting, and the scene is peaceful.

CLEVELAND'S BREATHTAKING SKYLINE. The Cleveland skyline and lakefront have changed dramatically through the years. It is winter here, and the partially frozen Lake Erie provides a dramatic backdrop for the high-rises claiming Cleveland skies. The black building on the left is the Frank Lausche Office Building. The first skyscraper appearing just in front of the Cleveland Browns Stadium is the Justice Center, in front of which is the nearly black Illuminating Company building. Next is the Terminal Tower, which still remains Cleveland's most recognizable landmark. It stands directly behind the low-rise buildings with an arched entrance that is known as Tower City. The tallest building in view is the Society Center Building. The second tallest skyscraper is the BP Building. On the right and to the back is Erieview Tower, and Gund Arena, home of the Cleveland Cavaliers, is to the right of center. Cleveland has maintained a population of just over 500,000 and will continue to strive to remain a wonderful place in which to live. (Photograph by David Kachinko.)

www.ingramcontent.com/pod-product-compliance
Lightning Source LLC
Chambersburg PA
CBHW080613110426
42813CB00006B/1498